LIFE INSURANCE:
Its Rate of Return

By

WILLIAM D. BROWNLIE

THE NATIONAL UNDERWRITER COMPANY
420 East Fourth Street
Cincinnati, Ohio 45202

Copyright 1983 by
WILLIAM D. BROWNLIE

All rights reserved.

No part of this book may be reproduced or transmitted in any form or by any means, electronic or mechanical, including photocopying, recording, or by any information storage and retrieval system, without the written permission of the publisher.

First Edition, August, 1983

Library of Congress Catalog Number 83-61584
International Standard Book Number 0-87218-033-6

Printed in the United States of America

DEDICATION

To my wife, Mary...

> who became my sounding board and who, after hearing me talk about the rate of return day in and day out, finally said to me, "Write like you talk; what you are writing should revolutionize the way life insurance will be bought and sold throughout the world."

To my children; Bill, Debby, Beth, Kate and Ted...

> you are my rate of return.

A QUICK NOTE

concerning the late William A. Steiger, Congressman from the State of Wisconsin, who was a member of the U.S. House of Representatives' Committee on Ways and Means.

(Congressman Steiger) "... you made me a believer in our system of government. You responded to a private citizen — one man, representing no one, who addressed an issue that he believed had to be corrected. You reinforced my belief that when you have something to say, say it. Thank you!"

William D. Brownlie

ACKNOWLEDGEMENTS

William Eugene Hays, CLU
Walter L. Downing, CLU
Raymond A. Desautels, CLU

> General Agents, New England Mutual
> Life Insurance Company

To Walt and Ray — and the late Gene Hays — thank you for your patience and for understanding my personality. Without each of you I could not have survived in the life insurance business.

William Kosinar, M.B.A.
Richard Garniewicz, M.B.A.

Thank you, Bill and Dick, for your thoughtful suggestions.

E.J. Moorhead, F.S.A.

Thank you, Jack, for your thoughtful answers to my many questions.

Mary Denise Dunn, B.S., M.Ed.

Thank you, Denise, for your assistance as my editor.

TABLE OF CONTENTS

1 Introductory Remarks 1

2 The Importance of the Rate of Return ... 5

3 Rate of Return Basics 15

4 Factors Influencing Your Decisions About Life Insurance 23

5 Existing Life Insurance: Should It Be Replaced or Exchanged? 33

6 A Discussion of Life Insurance Plans and Methods of Premium Payment 49

7 Explanation of the Brownlie Method of Calculations 55

8 Rate of Return for Life Insurance Plans Using the Brownlie Method of Calculations 61

9 Rate of Return for Methods of Premium
   Payment Using the Brownlie Method
   of Calculations 69

10 Introduction to the Hewlett-Packard 41-C
   Hand Calculator With Financial Decisions
   Module 77

11 How to Calculate the Rate of Return for
   Life Insurance Plans 91

12 How to Calculate the Rate of Return for
   Methods of Premium Payment 149

Appendix Test Yourself: Rate of Return
   Quizzes and Answers 189

EDITOR'S NOTE

The contents of this book will be controversial to some readers. Since life insurance and related areas are very complex subjects, each individual's situation must be dealt with separately and no generalizations should be construed as applicable to all cases. It is important, therefore, that your own situation be analyzed by a qualified life insurance agent.

Moreover, it is not the intention of the publisher or the author to offer legal, accounting or other professional advice. If such professional assistance is required, the services of a competent professional should be sought.

The principal source of the information presented here is the life insurance companies. Every effort has been made to be factually correct and free from error concerning the figures, illustrations and methods presented. Although carefully checked at all stages of production, error is possible. Neither The National Underwriter Company nor the author assume any responsibility for a loss or liability that may arise from the use of the applications or by any inaccuracy of the material found in this book.

While the author is heavily involved in financial planning for his clients, he continues to identify himself as a representative of New England Mutual Life and its affiliated companies. It should not be perceived that his company, New England Mutual Life, or any professional association to which he belongs, such as The Million Dollar Round Table, either endorses or sponsors his rate of return method.

1
INTRODUCTORY REMARKS

It is my personal opinion that an aura of mystery surrounds the rate of return on life insurance. This is an opinion based upon 25 years of experience in selling and servicing the life insurance needs of my clients. It is my aim to dispel this aura of mystery once and for all. To the best of my knowledge, no other book offered to the general public has addressed the rate of return the way I have. And, of equal importance, no other book has been written to show the public how to calculate the rate of return.

This book has not been written to discuss, comment on, or address any of the talk which may be heard in locker rooms, operating rooms, lunchrooms, at cocktail parties, bridge tables, or in boardrooms ... talk which says:

- "Term insurance is the only way to go."
- "Buy term, invest the difference."
- "Whole life insurance is dead!"
- "You don't need life insurance as you get older."
- "Why should I make my wife rich for her next husband?"
- "Universal Life is the greatest thing since they invented the wheel!"
- "You can invest your money better than the insurance company."
- "Don't buy life insurance as part of your Keogh and/or corporate retirement plan!"
- "The insurance companies do *not* want you to know the rate of return."
- "Don't worry about it. The government will take care of your wife!"

The ten comments just cited have been addressed, in one way or another, by various books, talk shows, TV specials and the 1979 *Staff Report to the Federal Trade Commission on Life Insurance Cost Disclosure.* This book has been written with one essential purpose in mind; to introduce the individual to the concept dealing with the rate of return on a life insurance policy from the beneficiary's point of view and from the insured's point of view.

I strongly believe this book should be read and used by certain groups of people. To which group do you belong?

- Life insurance agents who seek to educate their policyholders, and themselves, to understand the rate of return without the necessity of expensive computers.
- Millions of people who currently own life insurance and must be helped to understand what they are getting for their money.
- People who buy life insurance without any advice who will now have a tool — this book — to assist

Introductory Remarks

them in determining which type of life insurance is best for them.

- Financial advisors such as attorneys, accountants, bankers, trust officers, and financial planners who seek to acquire additional expertise in life insurance.

- Personnel directors and directors of fringe benefit programs who are constantly bombarded with various life insurance plans which provide post-retirement death benefits for selected employees of their respective companies.

- College professors and instructors of life insurance who will now have a book which will be easily understood by students and which will answer the question everybody should be asking: "What do people get for their money when they buy life insurance?"

- Students of life insurance who will have a book which tells them that the subject of life insurance need not be complex. Life insurance is predicated on basic training in the mathematics of finance, which is compound interest. The complicated areas of life insurance involve who is to own the policy and how the premium will be paid. In those areas one needs a highly skilled life insurance agent.

- Life insurance home office executives who should be reminded what the life insurance business is supposed to be about — the providing of a death benefit.

- Critics of life insurance who use rhetoric instead of facts. For those whose criticism has been aimed at the insured's rate of return, this book will remind them that the purpose of life insurance is to provide a death benefit. Therefore, it is the beneficiary's rate of return which must be examined.

- State insurance commissioners who should make consumers aware of the rate of return. Commissioners can help by offering this book, through their departments, to the citizens of their respective states in the same manner as *Buyers' Guides* have been offered by insurance commissioners' offices.

2

THE IMPORTANCE OF THE RATE OF RETURN

There is much confusion and disagreement about the rate of return as it applies to life insurance.

There are some who believe that to apply the term "rate of return" to the death benefit — what I would call the beneficiary's rate of return — is totally inappropriate. They believe it is not necessary to measure the beneficiary's rate of return.

There are some who believe that the only rate of return on a life insurance policy is the rate of return which the insured receives if the policy is surrendered.

There are some who believe that the only way to measure the insured's rate of return is to apply the Linton Yield Method.

Life Insurance: Its Rate of Return

There are some who believe that it is perfectly permissible to use the Linton Yield Method regarding the rate of return in any context.

I agree that the Linton Yield Method has its place; but I disagree with the indiscriminate use/application of the Linton Yield Method.

Those to whom I am referring know who they are. Rather than identify them publicly, I prefer to simply say, they are not life insurance agents.

My adversaries and I do agree on one point, however. That is, we all accept the basic premise that the essential purpose of life insurance is to provide a death benefit.

Why do I believe the term "rate of return" is appropriately used in conjunction with the beneficiary, and why is it essential to measure the beneficiary's rate of return?

Based upon years of experience in selling and servicing life insurance, it is my contention that it is essential for the life insurance agent and the policyholder to be constantly *reassured* that the death benefit cannot be duplicated in any other financial product. The only way to know whether or not the death benefit can be duplicated in another financial product is to know, at all times, what the rate of return is to the beneficiary. Those of us who sell and service life insurance cannot afford to assume anything.

I consider life insurance to be a financial transaction. Look at my personal situation. I pay premiums to New England Mutual Life with cold, hard-earned, negotiable American dollars, not with returnable bottles, homegrown vegetables or tickets to the Boston Celtics' games. When I die, New England Mutual Life will pay Mary Clare Brownlie cold, hard, negotiable American dollars. To me, the manner in which I pay and the manner in which Mary

The Importance of the Rate of Return

Clare Brownlie gets paid is *finance*. What Mary will get for my money is her return; her actual rate of return depends upon when I die.

What do I think about the insured's rate of return?

It is always important for one to know what he/she is getting for their money. To that extent Bill Brownlie, and anybody else who is paying for life insurance, should know what he would get back in the event the policy was surrendered. Notice what you have just read! *Unless* the policy is surrendered, there is no rate of return to the insured. Also, there is a rate of return to the insured only if the policy surrendered is on life insurance plans that are not term life insurance. The rate of return to the insured on term life insurance is always — 100% compound.

Although the availability of cash values to the insured is important, I still feel quite strongly that the actual rate of return on life insurance is the rate of return to the beneficiary. This belief is predicated on the universally accepted premise that the purpose of life insurance is to provide a death benefit.

What do I think about the Linton Yield Method?

The late M. Albert Linton, a distinguished actuary, created the Linton Yield Method in 1919. The Linton Yield Method provides a way of knowing what the rate of return is on the savings component of a whole life policy.

It is not a method which measures the rate of return to the beneficiary.

It is not a method which measures the actual, true, intrinsic rate of return to the insured, net after taxes, if the policy is surrendered.

The Linton Yield Method is a method based upon certain assumptions. The method indicates what a consumer would have to earn in interest if he bought term life insurance and invested the difference. This is in order to be as well off (from an investment viewpoint) as he would have been had he purchased whole life insurance.

In my opinion, the use of the Linton Yield Method should be limited to discussions which involve "buy term, invest the difference." Otherwise, misapplication results in an artificial inflation of the insured's rate of return.

Note to the reader: Keep in mind that the essential purpose of life insurance is to provide a death benefit ... the essential purpose of life insurance is to provide a death benefit ... the essential purpose of life insurance...

The Importance of the Rate of Return

Example: $100,000 Whole Life (Ordinary Life), Male, Age 35, Non-Cigarette Smokers Premium. Dividends, as declared, are used to reduce the premium.

A. *Rate of Return Based Upon Brownlie Method of Calculations*

Time Span	Present Value Payment (premium)	Cash Surrender Value
Yr 1	$1,301	0
Yr 2	1,242	1,215
Yr 3	1,183	2,438
Yr 4	1,120	3,699
Yr 5	1,055	4,997

The rate of return to the insured, if the policy is surrendered after five years, is minus 5.31% (−5.31%).

B. *Rate of Return Based Upon Linton Yield Method of Calculations*

Time Span	Yearly Renewable Term	Whole Life Premium	Term Premium	Present Value Payment	Investment Fund**
Yr 1	$100,000	$1,301	$175	$1,126	0
Yr 2	98,785	1,242	196	1,046	1,215
Yr 3	97,562	1,183	219	964	2,438
Yr 4	96,301	1,120	245	875	3,699
Yr 5	95,003	1,055	272	783	4,997

** Investment Fund is equal to the cash surrender value of a whole life policy.

Note: The Present Value Payment has been reduced by an assumed cost for term insurance. The death benefit is always $100,000. The death benefit is a combination of the Investment Fund and the face amount of the Yearly Renewable Term life insurance.

The rate of return to the insured, if the policy is surrendered after five years, is 1.31%.

In what context should the Linton Yield Method be used?

It is my opinion that the Linton Yield Method should only be used in a "buy term, invest the difference" discussion. It is also my opinion that the Linton Yield Method provides both the life insurance agent and the consumer with a benchmark in that context. The benchmark is what would have to be earned in compound interest on the invested difference in order for the consumer to be as well off as he would have been had he purchased whole life insurance.

In the preceding example, the consumer would have had to earn, net after taxes, 1.31% on the invested difference over a five-year period to be as well off.

Harold G. Ingraham, Jr.,[1] has provided the following figures based upon the example used.

Linton Yield Method is:

Time Span		
	10 yrs	8.61%
	15 yrs	9.52%
	30 yrs	9.98%
	45 yrs	10.11%

It becomes apparent from the viewpoints of whole life and term life insurance that the longer the insurance stays in force, the longer one has to earn a higher rate of compound interest, net after taxes. This is necessary in order to be as well off as one would have been if one had purchased whole life insurance.

What is the serious flaw of the Linton Yield Method?

The serious flaw of the Linton Yield Method is the use of an assumed term premium based on representative pre-

---

[1] Harold G. Ingraham, Jr., F.S.A., CLU, Senior Vice-president and Chief Actuary of New England Mutual Life.

The Importance of the Rate of Return

miums. In our example, the term cost is the cost for Yearly Renewable Term Life insurance, male, age 35, non-cigarette smokers premium, non-reissue for New England Life. Since there are no standard rates for term life insurance, the cost varies from company to company. New England Life's term life insurance rates are competitive, but it is unlikely they are the lowest available.

Do I have any evidence that life insurance companies share my views?

Yes, I have evidence. I call your attention to the January 31, 1983 issue of *Forbes*, page 98. There is an advertisement on that page placed by The Guardian Life Insurance Company of America. Carefully read the ad which is reproduced on page 12.

Excerpts from The Guardian Life advertisement...

LifeGuard Whole Life in Action:
LifeGuard Whole Life $100,000, Age 35, Male, Preferred Annual Premium: $1,531.00 Dividends used to Purchase paid-up Additions.

End of Year	Total Cash Value	Return on Investment	Return on Investment With Cost of Insurance
20	$ 85,302	8.99%	10.40%
Age 65	$264,433	9.77%	10.92%

Based upon the raw data supplied in this advertisement, the Brownlie Method of Calculations would have produced the same rates of return, 8.99% and 9.77%.

The returns of 10.40% and 10.92% are the Linton Yield Method calculations which are properly shown as separate from the return on the actual premium of $1,531.00 paid each and every year for 20 and 30 years.

Life Insurance: Its Rate of Return

"Whole Life Insurance? Reports of its death have been greatly exaggerated!"

Leo R. Futia, CLU
Chairman of the Board,
Guardian Life

Guardian's LifeGuard Whole Life is everything the critics said whole life insurance couldn't be. In fact, it's the most competitive blend of insurance protection and cash accumulation in our 122-year history.

This policy is backed by Guardian's superior financial strength and long-term investment strategy. Like all Guardian products, LifeGuard was developed with the safety and security of the policyholder foremost in mind.

Contact a Guardian agent for a personal illustration showing the results this policy can generate for you. When you see the numbers, you'll see just how much **life** there is in Guardian's **Whole Life**.

LifeGuard Whole Life in Action:
LifeGuard Whole Life, $100,000, Age 35, Male, Preferred
Annual Premium: $1,531.00   Dividends used to Purchase Additions

End of Year	Total Death Benefit*	Total Cash Value*	Return on Investment**	Return on Investment with Cost of Insurance†
20	$194,751	$ 85,302	8.99%	10.40%
Age 65	406,699	264,433	9.77%	10.92%

Guaranteed Cash Values: 20th year, $30,845; Age 65, $49,183

*Figures depending on dividends are neither estimated nor guaranteed, but are based on the dividend scale for 1983. A settlement dividend is paid upon death, surrender, or maturity, or upon continuation for reduced paid up or extended term insurance, provided that premiums have been paid for at least eleven years.

**The Return On Investment reflects the total cash value growth in relation to annual premium payments, and indicates the equivalent yield that an individual must earn in an alternate investment.

†The Return on Investment With Cost of Insurance reflects the total cash value growth in relation to annual premium payments, and indicates the equivalent yield that an individual must earn in an alternate investment, after deducting the annual cost of the insurance based on The Guardian's current Yearly Renewable Term rates for the age, face amount and policy class shown above.

Dividends are affected by policy loans. Under current economic conditions, in any given policy year, the greater the amount of loans, the smaller the dividend. The above illustration assumes no loans.

The Guardian Life Insurance Company of America
201 Park Avenue South, New York, NY 10003 • A mutual company established in 1860

The Importance of the Rate of Return

Do I have any evidence that the indiscriminate use of the Linton Yield Method has caused confusion, inaccurate results and/or misconceptions about life insurance?

Yes, I believe I do have such evidence! The 1979 *Staff Report to the Federal Trade Commission on Life Insurance Cost Disclosure* used the Linton Yield Method for purposes of arriving at rates of return on life insurance. In my opinion, this resulted in:

- an inaccurate (possibly inflated, but not a true, intrinsic) rate of return to the insured;
- a complete disregard of the beneficiary's rate of return;
- confusion of the public concerning the purpose of life insurance (which is to provide a death benefit) by the FTC's disregard of the beneficiary's rate of return;
- the FTC leading the public to believe they are not getting their money's worth out of life insurance.

Did the 1979 Staff Report to the Federal Trade Commission on Life Insurance Cost Disclosure provide any beneficial information to the public?

Yes. The report reconfirmed what I have always known. If you only need and want life insurance for a temporary period of time, you are better off buying term life insurance. If you buy a form of non-term life insurance — that is, Whole Life (Ordinary Life), Adjustable Premium Whole Life (Universal Life) or Variable Life — and drop the policy, you will lose a lot of money.

Non-term life insurance should only be purchased by those who want the life insurance to mature as a death benefit. Depending upon when one dies (statistically, half of us die before reaching our life expectancy, and half of us die after reaching our life expectancy) term life insurance could prove to be extremely inexpensive (if one dies

Life Insurance: Its Rate of Return

before reaching life expectancy) or extremely expensive (if one dies after reaching life expectancy).

The age-old question still remains: Tell me when you are going to die, and I will tell you which form of life insurance to buy!

I hope that in this chapter I have been clear enough so all of you truly grasp my thoughts, feelings, and opinions concerning the critical importance of understanding the rate of return on life insurance.

I hope that I have led you to understand that, in all times and in all situations, prudence dictates that you must remember the *primary* purpose of life insurance is to provide a death benefit.

I hope you now clearly understand what the rate of return is so you will know why I have written this book.

3
RATE OF RETURN BASICS

There are probably some of you who are thinking that I am just another life insurance agent trying to sell life insurance through this book. Guess what? You're dead wrong! My only purpose in writing this book is to educate people about the rate of return on life insurance, one of the realities of life. But, guess again! If you want to buy life insurance from me, I'll be more than happy to sell it to you.

Now, if you really do believe this book is written only to sell life insurance and not to educate people about the rate of return, then immediately return this book to the publisher for a prompt refund of your money. For those of you who truly want to learn about the rate of return on life insurance, read on. You won't be disappointed!

Life Insurance: Its Rate of Return

How should the rate of return be measured?

The rate of return is always measured in terms of compound interest. Separate measurements are used from the viewpoints of the beneficiary and of the insured. However, both measurements are in compound interest.

What is meant by compound interest?

Compound interest is a measurement which is universally accepted. For example, the chief executive officer of any *Fortune 500* company — or any firm, for that matter — will always measure corporate goals in terms of compound growth. Mutual funds, tax-shelters in real estate, oil and gas, common stocks, and the Consumer Price Index are all measured in terms of compound interest. Life insurance should also be measured in terms of compound interest return both to the beneficiary and to the insured.

What is the definition of compound interest?

Webster's New Collegiate Dictionary (1981 edition) defines compound interest as the "interest computed on the sum of an original principal and accrued interest."

> For example: You put $1.00 in the bank. Interest paid each and every year is always added to the original $1.00 *plus* previously paid interest. Therefore, $1.00 at 10% compound interest will grow to $2.59 in 10 years, $4.17 in 20 years, and $13,780.61 in 100 years.

Remember: Compound interest is a basic element of the mathematics of finance when you are seeking to measure the return on your money or when you are seeking to measure the return on money you have given someone else to produce for you. It is important to understand that

Rate of Return Basics

a 370% gain over the past decade is *not* 370% compound interest. In compound interest terms it is 16.73%. A 1,213% gain over 15 years is equal to 18.72% compound interest.

What is the essential purpose of life insurance?

The essential purpose of life insurance is to provide a death benefit for the beneficiary. Recognizing this essential purpose means you should consider the principal question: What would you, or your company, have to earn in compound interest in order to accumulate the same amount of money that the insurance company will pay your beneficiary at your death?

What does the rate of return on life insurance reveal?

If you accept the definition of the essential purpose of life insurance, as outlined above, then it is only logical that your primary concern should be the rate of return to the beneficiary.

A. Life insurance provides an extremely attractive return for the beneficiary. The return is so significant that it may be impossible, or at least extremely difficult, to duplicate the rate of return in any other financial product. This is particularly true during the first 20 years of the life of the policy or, perhaps, even longer, depending upon the particular plan of life insurance purchased.

Time works against the beneficiary. The longer the insured lives, the lower the rate of return to the beneficiary. However, depending upon the individual tax bracket, or the tax bracket of the company, (and as long as the Congress of the United States allows life insurance proceeds to be exempt from Federal Income Tax) it may continue to be difficult to duplicate in another financial product the compound interest return which the life insurance provides to the beneficiary.

B. Life insurance does not offer a significant rate of return to the insured on any plan in the early years of the policy. However, the longer the policy is in force, the rate of return to the insured increases significantly.

How can the rate of return be known?

All life insurance proposals should indicate the rate of return for both the beneficiary and the insured. All proposals should be accompanied by an official ledger statement produced by the computer service of the life insurance company. On the ledger statement are shown:

(a) the premium, year by year;
(b) the death benefit;
(c) the projected dividends;
(d) the terminal dividend;
(e) the total cash value; and
(f) the cash value and/or net equity.

Remember: The death benefit is always for the beneficiary. The cash value, total cash value, and/or net equity value is always for the insured. We have also assumed, for the purposes of this book, that the insured is also the policyholder.

What are some other ways to know the rate of return?

All life insurance companies have the capability to indicate the rate of return (for the beneficiary and for the insured) on their official ledger statements. Currently, few do; most do not.

The question becomes, "Do the life insurance companies wish to spend the money necessary to do so?" Equally

Rate of Return Basics

important is the question, "Do the life insurance companies wish to spend considerable amounts of money to indicate the rate of return for both the beneficiary and the insured on in force ledger statements for existing policyholders?"

The life insurance agent may be able to take an official ledger statement and calculate the rate of return. Some life insurance agents subscribe to independent computer facilities which provide the rates of return for both the beneficiary and the insured. This is done by storing in the computer the rates and values of most life insurance companies. It must be pointed out that these ledger statements are not official ledger statements of the life insurance companies and they do not provide rates of return on in force statements of existing policies.

For the purposes of this book, what is meant by rate of return terminology?

Present value payment ... the premium is referred to as the present value payment.
Future value ... the future value is a value to be received in the future by the beneficiary (the death benefit) or by the insured (the cash value, total cash value, and/or net equity value).
Time span ... the time span is the number of years over which you wish to measure the rate of return.

Where will you find present value payment, future value and time span?

In most cases, it is difficult to find present value payment, future value and time span on a year-by-year basis in the standard policy form issued by a life insurance company. The above terms will be found either on the official

Life Insurance: Its Rate of Return

ledger statement produced by the computer service of the life insurance company whose proposal is being considered, *or* on the in force ledger statement provided by many life insurance companies for existing policies.

Note: The importance of the official ledger statement produced by the computer service of the life insurance company cannot be overstated. You must *demand* an official ledger statement, not an extrapolated summary of an official ledger statement.

How is an official ledger statement comparable to the window sticker on a brand-new automobile?

When you buy a brand-new automobile, you will find on the window of the automobile a sticker which, by law, must be visible. That sticker completely describes the automobile you are going to buy. The sticker will tell you about the standard equipment, the accessories, the radio, the air-conditioning, and so forth. In other words, the sticker describes the anatomy of the car you are going to buy. In exactly the same way, the official ledger statement produced by the computer service of the life insurance company describes the anatomy of the life insurance plan and/or method of premium payment under consideration for purchase; *or* the life insurance policy under consideration for replacement or exchange.

What determines the rate of return?

The rate of return is determined by: the present value payment (the premium); the future value (death benefit to the beneficiary, cash value, total cash value, and/or net equity value to the insured); and the time span (number of years paid).

Why is life insurance self-contained compound interest?

The compound interest return for the beneficiary and for the insured is self-contained within the life insurance policy. This is very important! Many investment products deliver a return which then must be reinvested elsewhere in order to actually realize a given level of compound return.

4

FACTORS INFLUENCING YOUR DECISIONS ABOUT LIFE INSURANCE

In addition to the reality concerning the rate of return, there are other factors which may influence your perceptions and your decisions about life insurance. Some of these factors may relate to age, income, tax deductions, and tax advantages.

Certain facts about America's population are becoming obvious. The percentage of older citizens is growing larger

Life Insurance: Its Rate of Return

all the time. People are living longer and, therefore, must plan prudently for old age. Inflation is here to stay; taxes will not go away; Social Security is unsettled. The older citizen must remember that Group Term Life Insurance terminates at retirement which makes post-retirement death benefits essential. Because of all these factors, it is my opinion that life insurance must have a permanent place in all prudent, farsighted financial planning.

Remember: If you have chosen to terminate a life insurance policy on your life, then at your death the rate of return is *zero* (0) to the beneficiary. The rate of return to you on premiums paid before and up to the termination of the policy is minus (−) 100% compound for term insurance. Your rate of return on other plans of life insurance will depend upon the rate of return as measured by the present value payment, the future value (either cash value, total cash value, and/or net equity) and the time span up to the point of termination.

How difficult is it to achieve a significant rate of return?

Do not be naive enough to believe all the talk — that is, the locker room, operating room, cocktail party, lunchroom, bridge table, and boardroom patter and chatter — that claims it is easy to achieve a significant rate of return on money invested outside of life insurance. Eventually, the talk continues, you will become self-insured and you will no longer need life insurance to provide a death benefit.

From my professional experience as a licensed life insurance advisor (Commonwealth of Massachusetts, Department of Banking and Insurance, Division of Insurance) and as a registered representative of New England Life Equity Services Corporation, Broker-Dealer (a wholly owned subsidiary of New England Mutual Life), I am acutely aware of just how difficult it is to achieve a significant rate of return on a consistent basis, net after taxes. Additionally, through my close association with New England Mutual Life, I have access to their affiliate, Loomis-Sayles (the distinguished Boston investment counseling firm) which provides me with a valuable source of current thinking concerning the developments in the money markets. Obviously then, I do have a very firm and very experienced basis on which to state that my opinion is that of other experts; it is very, very difficult to consistently achieve a significant rate of return, net after taxes. I offer as further evidence the following comparison of Compound Return Indexes.

Bond & Equity Market Indexes — 12/31/82[1]

	10 Years	5 Years	1982
Consumer Price Index	8.8%	9.6%	4.6%
91-Day Treasury Bills	8.5	10.8	10.7
Standard & Poor 500	6.7	14.0	21.5
Dow Jones Industrials	5.8	11.3	27.2
New York Stock Exchange	2.3	9.1	14.0
Value Line Composite	3.4	11.1	15.3
AMEX Indicator Digest	11.7	29.7	36.8
Europe, Australia, Far East Stock Exchanges	7.1	11.7	–0.8
Lehman Government/Corporate Bond	7.5	8.4	31.1
Salomon Bros. High-Grade Long-Term Corporate Bond Index	6.1	5.8	43.7

[1] Source: A.G. Becker, Inc. Reprinted with permission.

After studying the Compound Return Indexes, think for a moment. Have your investments for the past ten years, or the past five years, or for 1982, given you a rate of return of 8.8%, 9.6%, or 4.6%? If they have, you are just running even with the Consumer Price Index (the inflation rate).

Economists tell us that an acceptable rate of return on investments is 2% to 4% above the inflation rate. In order

Life Insurance: Its Rate of Return

for you to be ahead of the inflation rate, you would have to have had a rate of return of:

10 years	Rate of Return	10.8% — 12.8%
5 years	Rate of Return	11.6% — 13.6%
1982	Rate of Return	6.6% — 8.6%

How is it that life insurance may be considered "money down the road" for the insured?

An astute investor recently said to me, "Let me tell you why I bought life insurance. I didn't need it. I wasn't married at the time I bought it. And, when I did get married, we didn't have any children and we do not intend to have any children. I bought life insurance because I knew it would be money down-the-road. And, if I didn't buy life insurance, I would have blown the money." The "money down the road" is the cash surrender value which this wise investor knows will always be there whenever he wants it, or whenever he needs it.

Why is life insurance a tax shelter for the beneficiary?

Life insurance is a tax shelter for the beneficiary because Section 101(2) of the Internal Revenue Code provides for life insurance proceeds to be received by the beneficiary completely exempt from Federal Income Tax. A 112.33% compound interest return to the beneficiary is equal to a 187.21% compound interest rate of return. For a 40% bracket taxpayer to duplicate the death benefit for the beneficiary in another financial product (i.e. bonds, mutual funds, money market funds, common stock), a compound return of 187.21% would have to be achieved on the money otherwise paid in premiums. The only exception to this would be if it were possible to find a 112.33% rate of return from a tax-exempt bond. The rate of return of 112.33% is the compound interest rate of return on the fifth year death benefit for $100,000 Whole Life (Ordinary

Factors Influencing Your Decisions

Life) using dividends, as declared, to reduce the premium for a male, age 35. This return is predicated on premiums paid within the time span of five years.

Why is life insurance a tax-deferred plan for the insured?

Under current law, the cash value is allowed to accumulate tax-deferred within the policy. This means the insured will pay no tax on the cash value until the policy is actually terminated. At that time, there is a tax due only if the cash surrender value (and/or total cash value and/or net equity) is greater than what has been paid for the policy. Loans against the cash value do not result in a tax *unless* or *until* the policy is actually terminated. Again, the tax will be due ONLY if the value received exceeds what was paid for the policy.

What is meant by tax-deductible life insurance?

There are many ways in which life insurance may be purchased on a tax-deductible basis. This means that the present value payment (the premium) can be reduced because it can be tax-deductible. The future value (either the death benefit to the beneficiary or the cash value, total cash value and/or net equity value to the insured) may be subject, wholly or partially, to Federal Income Tax depending upon which section of the Internal Revenue Code governs your tax-deductible plan. This tax fact must be taken into consideration when calculating the rate of return for the particular tax-deductible plan you are considering.

What are the ways in which life insurance can be purchased on a tax-deductible basis?

- Unincorporated Retirement Plan (Keogh Plan, subject to PS-58 cost);

Life Insurance: Its Rate of Return

Federal Income Tax Table*
Individuals, Estates and Trusts
(Tax Years Beginning in 1983)

Col. 1 Taxable Income $	Separate Return Tax on Col. 1 $	Rate on Excess %	Joint Return Tax on Col. 1 $	Rate on Excess %	Single Return Tax on Col. 1 $	Rate on Excess %	Head of Household Tax on Col. 1 $	Rate on Excess %	Trusts and Estates Tax on Col. 1 $	Rate on Excess %
...	...	0	...	0	...	0	...	0	...	11
1,050	...	0	...	0	...	0	...	0	115	13
1,700	...	11	...	0	...	0	...	0	200	13
2,100	44	11	...	0	...	0	...	0	252	15
2,300	66	11	...	0	...	11	...	11	282	15
2,750	115	13	...	0	50	11	50	11	350	15
3,400	200	13	...	11	121	13	121	11	447	15
3,800	252	15	44	11	173	13	165	11	507	15
4,250	320	15	94	11	232	13	215	11	574	17
4,400	342	15	110	11	251	15	231	13	600	17
5,500	507	15	231	13	416	15	374	13	787	17
5,950	574	17	290	13	484	15	433	13	863	17
6,300	634	17	335	13	536	15	478	13	923	19
6,500	668	17	361	13	566	15	504	15	961	19
7,600	855	17	504	15	731	15	669	15	1,170	19
8,000	923	19	564	15	791	15	729	15	1,246	19
8,400	999	19	624	15	851	15	789	15	1,322	23
8,500	1,018	19	639	15	866	17	804	15	1,345	23
8,700	1,056	19	669	15	900	17	834	18	1,391	23
10,100	1,322	23	879	15	1,138	17	1,086	18	1,713	23
10,600	1,437	23	954	15	1,223	17	1,176	18	1,828	26
10,800	1,483	23	984	15	1,257	19	1,212	18	1,880	26
11,800	1,713	23	1,134	15	1,447	19	1,392	19	2,140	26
11,900	1,736	23	1,149	17	1,466	19	1,411	19	2,166	26
12,300	1,828	26	1,217	17	1,542	19	1,487	19	2,270	26
12,900	1,984	26	1,319	17	1,656	21	1,601	19	2,426	26
13,250	2,075	26	1,379	17	1,730	21	1,668	19	2,517	30
14,950	2,517	30	1,668	17	2,087	21	1,991	19	3,027	30
15,000	2,532	30	1,676	17	2,097	24	2,000	21	3,042	30
15,900	2,802	30	1,829	17	2,313	24	2,189	21	3,312	35
16,000	2,832	30	1,846	19	2,337	24	2,210	21	3,347	35
17,600	3,312	35	2,150	19	2,721	24	2,546	21	3,907	35
18,200	3,522	35	2,264	19	2,865	28	2,672	25	4,117	35
20,200	4,222	35	2,644	23	3,425	28	3,172	25	4,817	35
21,200	4,572	35	2,874	23	3,705	28	3,422	25	5,167	40
22,900	5,167	40	3,265	23	4,181	28	3,847	25	5,847	40
23,500	5,407	40	3,403	23	4,349	32	3,997	29	6,087	40
24,600	5,847	40	3,656	26	4,701	32	4,316	29	6,527	40
28,300	7,327	40	4,618	26	5,885	32	5,389	29	8,007	44
28,800	7,527	40	4,748	26	6,045	36	5,534	34	8,227	44
29,900	7,967	40	5,034	30	6,441	36	5,908	34	8,711	44
30,000	8,007	44	5,064	30	6,477	36	5,942	34	8,755	44
34,100	9,811	44	6,294	30	7,953	40	7,336	37	10,559	44
35,200	10,295	44	6,624	35	8,393	40	7,743	37	11,043	44
41,100	12,891	44	8,689	35	10,753	40	9,926	37	13,639	48
41,500	13,067	44	8,829	35	10,913	45	10,074	37	13,831	48
42,800	13,639	48	9,284	35	11,498	45	10,555	37	14,455	48
44,700	14,551	48	9,949	35	12,353	45	11,258	44	15,367	48
45,800	15,079	48	10,334	40	12,848	45	11,742	44	15,895	48
53,000	18,535	48	13,214	40	16,088	45	14,910	44	19,351	50
54,700	19,351	50	13,894	40	16,853	45	15,658	44	20,201	50
55,300	19,651	50	14,134	40	17,123	50	15,922	44	20,501	50
60,000	22,001	50	16,014	44	19,473	50	17,990	44	22,851	50
60,600	22,301	50	16,278	44	19,773	50	18,254	48	23,151	50
79,500	31,751	50	24,594	44	29,223	50	27,326	48	32,601	50
81,200	32,601	50	25,342	44	30,073	50	28,142	48	33,451	50
81,800	32,901	50	25,606	44	30,373	50	28,430	50	33,751	50
85,600	34,801	50	27,278	48	32,273	50	30,330	50	35,651	50
106,000	45,001	50	37,070	48	42,473	50	40,530	50	45,851	50
107,700	45,851	50	37,886	48	43,323	50	41,380	50	46,701	50
108,300	46,151	50	38,174	48	43,623	50	41,680	50	47,001	50
109,400	46,701	50	38,702	50	44,173	50	42,230	50	47,551	50

*This table reflects the appropriate zero bracket amounts. Certain taxpayers using this table must make special adjustments: e.g., taxpayers who itemize deductions, taxpayers who can be claimed as dependents, some married taxpayers filing separately, and taxpayers calculating tax on lump sum distributions.

Factors Influencing Your Decisions

Federal Income Tax Table*
Individuals, Estates and Trusts
*(Tax Years Beginning after 1983**)*

Col. 1 Taxable Income $	Separate Return Tax on Col. 1 $	Rate on Excess %	Joint Return Tax on Col. 1 $	Rate on Excess %	Single Return Tax on Col. 1 $	Rate on Excess %	Head of Household Tax on Col. 1 $	Rate on Excess %	Trusts and Estates Tax on Col. 1 $	Rate on Excess %
...	...	0	...	0	...	0	...	0	...	11
1,050	...	0	...	0	...	0	...	0	115	12
1,700	...	11	...	0	...	0	...	0	193	12
2,100	44	11	...	0	...	0	...	0	241	14
2,300	66	11	...	0	...	11	...	11	269	14
2,750	115	12	...	0	50	11	50	11	332	14
3,400	193	12	...	11	121	12	121	11	423	14
3,800	241	14	44	11	169	12	165	11	479	14
4,250	304	14	94	11	223	12	215	11	542	16
4,400	325	14	110	11	241	14	231	12	566	16
5,500	479	14	231	12	395	14	363	12	742	16
5,950	542	16	285	12	458	14	417	12	814	16
6,300	598	16	327	12	507	14	459	12	870	18
6,500	630	16	351	12	535	15	483	14	906	18
7,600	806	16	483	14	700	15	637	14	1,104	18
8,000	870	18	539	14	760	15	693	14	1,176	18
8,400	942	18	595	14	820	15	749	14	1,248	22
8,500	960	18	609	14	835	16	763	14	1,270	22
8,700	996	18	637	14	867	16	791	17	1,314	22
10,100	1,248	22	833	14	1,091	16	1,029	17	1,622	22
10,600	1,358	22	903	14	1,171	16	1,114	17	1,732	25
10,800	1,402	22	931	14	1,203	18	1,148	17	1,782	25
11,800	1,622	22	1,071	14	1,383	18	1,318	18	2,032	25
11,900	1,644	22	1,085	16	1,401	18	1,336	18	2,057	25
12,300	1,732	25	1,149	16	1,473	18	1,408	18	2,157	25
12,900	1,882	25	1,245	16	1,581	20	1,516	18	2,307	25
13,250	1,969	25	1,301	16	1,651	20	1,579	18	2,395	28
14,950	2,395	28	1,573	16	1,991	20	1,885	18	2,871	28
15,000	2,409	28	1,581	16	2,001	23	1,894	20	2,885	28
15,900	2,661	28	1,725	16	2,208	23	2,074	20	3,137	33
16,000	2,689	28	1,741	18	2,231	23	2,094	20	3,170	33
17,600	3,137	33	2,029	18	2,599	23	2,414	20	3,698	33
18,200	3,335	33	2,137	18	2,737	26	2,534	24	3,896	33
20,200	3,995	33	2,497	22	3,257	26	3,014	24	4,556	33
21,200	4,325	33	2,717	22	3,517	26	3,254	24	4,886	38
22,900	4,886	38	3,091	22	3,959	26	3,662	24	5,532	38
23,500	5,114	38	3,223	22	4,115	30	3,806	28	5,760	38
24,600	5,532	38	3,465	25	4,445	30	4,114	28	6,178	38
28,300	6,938	38	4,390	25	5,555	30	5,150	28	7,584	42
28,800	7,128	38	4,515	25	5,705	34	5,290	32	7,794	42
29,900	7,546	38	4,790	28	6,079	34	5,642	32	8,256	42
30,000	7,584	42	4,818	28	6,113	34	5,674	32	8,298	42
34,100	9,306	42	5,966	28	7,507	38	6,986	35	10,020	42
35,200	9,768	42	6,274	33	7,925	38	7,371	35	10,482	42
41,100	12,246	42	8,221	33	10,167	38	9,436	35	12,960	45
41,500	12,414	42	8,353	33	10,319	42	9,576	35	13,140	45
42,800	12,960	45	8,782	33	10,865	42	10,031	35	13,725	45
44,700	13,815	45	9,409	33	11,663	42	10,696	42	14,580	45
45,800	14,310	45	9,772	38	12,125	42	11,158	42	15,075	45
53,000	17,550	45	12,508	38	15,149	42	14,182	42	18,315	49
54,700	18,315	49	13,154	38	15,863	42	14,896	42	19,148	49
55,300	18,609	49	13,382	38	16,115	48	15,148	42	19,442	49
60,000	20,912	49	15,168	42	18,371	48	17,122	42	21,745	49
60,600	21,206	49	15,420	42	18,659	48	17,374	45	22,039	49
79,500	30,467	49	23,358	42	27,731	48	25,879	45	31,300	50
81,200	31,300	50	24,072	42	28,547	48	26,644	45	32,150	50
81,800	31,600	50	24,324	42	28,835	50	26,914	48	32,450	50
85,600	33,500	50	25,920	45	30,735	50	28,738	48	34,350	50
106,000	43,700	50	35,100	45	40,935	50	38,530	48	44,550	50
107,700	44,550	50	35,865	45	41,785	50	39,346	48	45,400	50
108,300	44,850	50	36,135	45	42,085	50	39,634	50	45,700	50
109,400	45,400	50	36,630	49	42,635	50	40,184	50	46,250	50
161,300	71,350	50	62,061	49	68,585	50	66,134	50	72,200	50
162,400	71,900	50	62,600	50	69,135	50	66,684	50	72,750	50

*This table reflects the appropriate zero bracket amounts. Certain taxpayers using this table must make special adjustments: e.g., taxpayers who itemize deductions, taxpayers who can be claimed as dependents, some married taxpayers filing separately, and taxpayers calculating tax on lump sum distributions.

**Beginning in 1985, this table will be adjusted for inflation. IRC Sec. 1(f).

- Incorporated Retirement Plan (Corporate Pension and/or Profit Sharing Plan, subject to PS-58 cost);
- Retired Lives Reserve (subject to Table I cost);
- IRC Section 79, Group Term Life Insurance (subject to Table I cost);
- Life Insurance owned and payable to an institution and/or entity whereby the premium paid is considered a charitable contribution;
- IRC Section 501(c)(9) Trust (subject to Table I cost).

What is meant by "PS-58 cost"?

PS-58 refers to Pension Service 58 of the Internal Revenue Service which has the cost of insurance protection to be included in the individual's gross income for tax purposes.

What is meant by "Table I cost"?

Section 79 of the Internal Revenue Code is the section devoted exclusively to Group Term Life Insurance. Here you will find the amount of group life insurance whose cost can be excluded from gross income. Table I determines the cost of insurance protection in excess of $50,000 which is taxable to the covered active employee before retirement.

What types of life insurance plans can be purchased tax advantageously in certain business situations?

- Split Dollar
- Death Benefit Only Plan
- Key Person Life Insurance
- Deferred Compensation
- Corporate Purchase
- Professional Corporate Purchase

Factors Influencing Your Decisions

After considering all the data in this chapter, and because of your unique insight into your personal situation, you may decide that the rate of return is not the only criterion to be used when you are considering the purchase of life insurance. Things may not work out the way you had planned. You may want and need life insurance for a longer period of time than you originally thought was necessary. You may settle for a lower rate of return for your beneficiary so that you will only have to pay premiums for a limited period of time, or not at all.

If you want to pay life insurance premiums for a limited period of time, then the life insurance plan you must choose is Whole Life (Ordinary Life) to be paid for on a Premium Offset/Vanishing Premium basis.[2]

If you want to have your premiums reduced every year and, eventually, pay no premium at all, then the life insurance plan you must choose is Whole Life (Ordinary Life) using dividends, as declared, to reduce the premiums.

It is also possible to achieve the results outlined above on an Adjustable Premium Whole Life (generically referred to as Universal Life) insurance plan.

Limiting premiums for a specified period of time and/or total elimination of premiums cannot be realized on Variable Life insurance plans that are currently being offered. However, when Adjustable Premium Variable Life (generically referred to as Universal Variable Life) becomes available, flexibility with premium payments will be realized.

Whole Life (Ordinary Life), Adjustable Premium Whole Life (Universal Life) and Variable Life, generally speaking, produce lower rates of return to the beneficiary than does Yearly Renewable Term Life insurance prior to reaching life expectancy. At or beyond life expectancy, these plans

[2] Chapter 9 has an explanation and example of this premium method.

produce a higher rate of return to the beneficiary than does Yearly Renewable Term Life insurance. Remember the age-old question which I have previously mentioned: Tell me when you are going to die and I'll tell you what plan of life insurance to buy. Also remember, Yearly Renewable Term Life insurance premiums must be paid each and every year in order to keep the life insurance in force.

In addition, Whole Life (Ordinary Life), Adjustable Premium Whole Life (Universal Life) and Variable Life provide other advantages. Some of these advantages are:

- the ability to borrow against the cash value of Whole Life (Ordinary Life);
- the ability to borrow against the cash value and/or withdraw the cash value without borrowing on Adjustable Premium Whole Life (Universal Life);

Note: The actual cash value of Adjustable Premium Whole Life (Universal Life) will depend upon the actual interest credited by the life insurance company.

- the ability to borrow against the cash value of Variable Life.

Note: The actual cash value of Variable Life will depend upon the actual investment performance of the portfolio.

Another important factor for you to consider is whether to replace or exchange existing life insurance policies. This is such a complex subject that I have devoted the next chapter to the question. With such a comprehensive explanation, it is my hope that the issue of replacement and/or exchange will be clarified for you.

5

EXISTING LIFE INSURANCE: SHOULD IT BE REPLACED OR EXCHANGED?

Do not be misled by all the glib talk about replacement or exchange of existing life insurance policies. Do not be influenced by volatile interest rates which will not go on forever. At one point, in the very recent past, interest rates were up to 18%. At the time of this writing, the prime rate is down to 10.5%.

What does it mean to replace an existing life insurance policy?

In my opinion, to replace an existing life insurance policy means to terminate the existing policy with one company and replace it with another life insurance policy from a different company.

What does it mean to exchange an existing life insurance policy?

In my opinion, to exchange an existing life insurance policy means to terminate the existing policy and replace it with another policy from the same life insurance company.

What does the rate of return have to do with replacing or exchanging an existing life insurance policy?

I believe that when the rate of return to the beneficiary or the insured, or to both, can be increased, replacement or exchange of existing life insurance policies should be considered.

What "tools" are needed to determine whether or not the rate of return can be increased?

You will need two "tools" to determine whether or not the rate of return can be increased. These two "tools" are:
(1) the official ledger statement for the existing policy which is referred to as the in force ledger statement; and
(2) the official ledger statement of the proposed policy.

What do you do with these two official ledger statements?

Once you have obtained the official ledger statements, you must calculate the rate of return from the present time to a future point in time using the figures from each of the official ledger statements.

Life Insurance: Replaced or Exchanged?

Note: Only you can determine the "future point in time." You may choose to measure 5 years, 10 years, or 20 years down-the-road. The number of years is up to you.

What are the variables which enter into a rate of return comparison when one is considering replacing or exchanging an existing policy?

There are two variables which must enter into the rate of return comparison. The first of these two variables is the interest rate which is going to be assumed on the cash surrender value of the existing policy.

The second of these two variables is the dividend projection on the life insurance company's official ledger statement. These dividends are not guaranteed. They are only projections and estimates into the future. When you are considering life insurance which pays dividends (not all life insurance companies pay dividends) make very sure that you investigate the integrity of the life insurance company. Is there evidence which indicates the life insurance company has always paid the dividend it projected? Is there evidence the life insurance company has paid a higher dividend then it projected?

The money derived from the replaced or exchanged policy is called the cash surrender value. Once the existing policy is replaced or exchanged, that money is available to the insured for immediate investment. When combined with the new policy, that money produces the total rate of return. The total rate of return must then be compared to the rate of return on the existing policy.

For purposes of comparison, what is a reasonable interest rate to assume for 1983?

It seems to me that a 10% interest rate for 1983 is both reasonable and conservative. In recent years, no expert

Life Insurance: Its Rate of Return

has been able to accurately predict the interest rate. We have witnessed dramatic and unpredictable swings of the prime rate, short-term rates and the Federal Discount Rate, just to name a few.

Factual evidence indicates that for the past ten years the inflation rate has been averaging 8.8% compound. If the inflation rate for the next ten years continues to average 8.8% compound, then a 10% compound return, particularly on a short-term interest basis (that is, money that matures in one year or less), should be able to be realized.

Remember: In most situations, the interest rate is predicated on the anticipated inflation rate plus points which insure a profit to the lender.

In addition to the rate of return, what other factors should be considered by the policyholder before replacing or exchanging an existing policy?

- The policyholder must agree that the interest rate assumed on the cash surrender value is realistic and can be attained over the period of time used in the rate of return comparison.
- The policyholder must be aware that if the existing policy is replaced, a new period of contestability starts. This period of contestability ranges from one to two years, depending upon the life insurance company.
- The policyholder should ask the life insurance agent *before* finalizing the exchange whether or not the incontestability carries over from the existing policy to the exchanged policy.
- The policyholder should be aware that if the cash surrender value exceeds the premiums paid, generally there is an ordinary income tax on the difference.

- The policyholder should ask what the underwriting requirements are for replaced policies. Replaced policies usually require an up-to-date physical examination. In addition to this physical examination, and depending upon the amount of life insurance involved, other requirements may be mandated. Additional requirements may include stress tests, current EKG, current chest x-ray, and so forth.
- The policyholder should ask what the underwriting requirements are for exchanged policies. Exchanged policies usually require only a short form health statement.
- The policyholder should *not* replace or exchange an existing policy until the new policy is issued as applied for, and a premium is paid placing the new policy in force.

Note: Four (4) case studies follow which offer concrete facts and figures. These case studies are offered to help you become familiar with the process of comparing rates of return between existing policies and proposed policies. These case studies have not taken taxes into consideration.

Life Insurance: Its Rate of Return

CASE STUDY #1

A 56-year-old male purchased $20,000 of life insurance as part of his Keogh Plan when he was 51-years-old. The premium is $648.20.

In Force Ledger Statement Indicates:

Death Benefit	Age 65	$20,000
Death Benefit	70	21,990
Total Cash Value	Age 65	$ 7,973
Total Cash Value	70	12,492
Current Cash Value		$ 3,105

Present Value Payments in Order to Calculate the Rate of Return To Age 65 and Age 70

$3,105 + $648.20 = $3,753.20 (present value payment)
Every year thereafter = 648.20 (present value payment)

Rate of Return	Age 65	Age 70
Insured:	−1.79%	0.28%
Beneficiary:	14.10%	6.25%

COMPARE WITH PROPOSED POLICY

$20,000 Whole Life
  $696 premium paid for 10 years. After 10 years dividends pay premiums.

Ledger Statement Indicates:

		Current	C.V. @ 10%	When Combined
Death Benefit	Age 65	$22,332	$ 7,321	$29,653
Death Benefit	70	21,812	11,791	33,603
Total Cash Value	Age 65	5,594	7,321	12,915
Total Cash Value	70	8,089	11,791	19,880

Note: Present value payment of $3,105 (cash surrender value of the existing policy) at 10% will grow to $7,321.43 in 9 years (Age 65) and to $11,791.23 in 14 years (Age 70).

Present Value Payments in Order to Calculate the Rate of Return To Age 65 and Age 70

$3,105 + $696.00 = $3,801.00 (present value payment)
2nd to 10th years = 696.00 (present value payment each and every year for 9 years)

Rate of Return	Age 65	Age 70
Insured:	5.05%	6.28%
Beneficiary:	18.11%	11.17%

Life Insurance: Its Rate of Return

CASE STUDY #2

A 56-year-old male purchased $100,000 of Whole Life on a personal basis when he was 51-years-old. Dividends as declared are purchasing one-year term insurance equal to the cash value; the balance is used to reduce premiums. Gross premium is $3,273.

In Force Ledger Statement Indicates:

Death Benefit	Age 65	$129,400
Death Benefit	70	142,080
Total Cash Value	Age 65	$ 29,400
Total Cash Value	70	41,387
Current Cash Value		$ 9,031

Present Value Payments in Order to Calculate the Rate of Return To Age 65 and Age 70

$9,031 + $3,115 = $12,146 (present value payment)
2nd to 14th year = 3,096, 3,091, 3,089, 3,013, 2,883, 2,832, 2,783, 2,773, 2,700, 2,812, 2,934, 3,062 (present value payments)

Rate of Return	Age 65	Age 70
Insured:	−3.18%	−2.18%
Beneficiary:	20.98%	11.31%

COMPARE WITH PROPOSED POLICY

$100,000 Whole Life
$3,379 premium paid for 9 years. After 9 years, dividends pay premium.

Ledger Statement Indicates:

		Current	C.V. @ 10%	When Combined
Death Benefit	Age 65	$111,660	$14,010	$125,670
Death Benefit	70	102,431	17,880	120,311
Total Cash Value	Age 65	$27,971	$14,010	41,981
Total Cash Value	70	36,456	17,880	54,336

Note: Present value payment of $9,031 (cash surrender value of the existing policy) at 5%, net after taxes, will grow to $14,010 in 9 years (Age 65) and to $17,880 in 14 years (Age 70).

Present Value Payments in Order to Calculate the Rate of Return To Age 65 and Age 70

$9,031 + $3,379 = $12,410 (present value payment)
2nd to 9th years = 3,379 (present value payment each and every year for 9 years)

Rate of Return	Age 65	Age 70
Insured:	1.05%	2.95%
Beneficiary:	19.31%	10.38%

CASE STUDY #3

A 60-year-old male purchased $57,502 of life insurance as part of his corporate pension plan when he was 53-years-old. Dividends as declared are used to reduce the premium. Gross premium is $2,666.77. Current net premium is $2,203.

In Force Ledger Statement Indicates:

Death Benefit	Age 65	$57,502
Death Benefit	70	57,502
Total Cash Value	Age 65	$17,552
Total Cash Value	70	24,775
Current Cash Value		$11,299

Present Value Payments in Order to Calculate the Rate of Return To Age 65 and Age 70

$11,299 + $2,203 = $13,502 (present value payment)
2nd to 10th years = 2,139, 2,088, 2,029, 1,966, 1,717, 1,622, 1,551, 1,498, 1,439 (present value payments)

Rate of Return	Age 65	Age 70
Insured:	–5.17%	–2.36%
Beneficiary:	25.68%	8.87%

Life Insurance: Replaced or Exchanged?

COMPARE WITH PROPOSED POLICY

$57,502 Whole Life
$2,384 premium for first 5 years; $2,284 premium for the next 4 years (premium waiver ended). After 9 years, dividends pay premium.

Ledger Statement Indicates:		*Current*	*C.V. @10%*	*When Combined*
Death Benefit	Age 65	$59,964	$18,197	$78,161
Death Benefit	70	64,974	29,306	94,280
Total Cash Value	Age 65	$ 8,404	$18,197	$26,601
Total Cash Value	70	20,090	29,306	49,396

Note: Present value payment of $11,299 (cash surrender value of the existing policy) at 10% will grow to $18,197.15 in 5 years (Age 65) and to $29,306.70 in 10 years (Age 70).

Present Value Payments in Order to Calculate the Rate of Return to Age 65 and Age 70

$11,299 + $2,384	=	$13,683	(present value payment)
2nd to 5th years	=	2,384	(present value payment)
6th to 9th years	=	2,254	(present value payment)

Rate of Return	*Age 65*	*Age 70*
Insured:	3.45%	5.70%
Beneficiary:	33.29%	14.47%

Life Insurance: Its Rate of Return

CASE STUDY #4

A 48-year-old male purchased $25,000 of life insurance when he was 36-years-old as part of his Keogh Plan. Dividends as declared are accumulating at interest with the insurance company. The premium is $596.00. At age 44, he purchased $132,392 of life insurance. Dividends as declared are buying supplemental life insurance. The premium is $2,601.00.

In Force Ledger Statement Indicates:

Death Benefit	$ 25,000	Policy	Age 65	$ 29,680
Death Benefit	132,392	Policy	65	149,153
Total Cash Value	$ 25,000	Policy	Age 65	$ 18,530
Total Cash Value	132,392	Policy	65	70,807
Current Combined Cash Value			$ 14,307	

Present Value Payments in Order to Calculate the Rate of Return To Age 65 and Age 70

$14,307 + $2,601 + $596   = $17,504   (present value payment)

   2nd to 17th years
   $2,601 + $596   =   3,197   (present value payment)

Rate of Return	Age 65
Insured:	2.42%
Beneficiary:	8.46%

Life Insurance: Replaced or Exchanged?

COMPARE WITH PROPOSED POLICY

$200,000 Adjustable Premium Whole Life (Universal Life)
$ 3,504 premium 1st year; $3,420 premium 2nd to 10th years.

Note: Based upon the current interest assumption of 10%, which is what the life insurance company is currently crediting, premiums only have to be paid for 10 years in order to have enough money to keep the insurance in force until age 95.

Ledger Statement Indicates:	Current	C.V. @ 10%	When Combined
Death Benefit	Age 65 $200,000	$72,314	$272,314
Total Cash Value	Age 65 $50,137	$72,314	$122,451

Note: Present value payment of $14,307 (cash surrender value of the existing policy) at 10% will grow to $72,314.31 in 17 years (Age 65).

Present Value Payments in Order to Calculate the Rate of Return To Age 65

$14,307 + $3,504   = $17,811 (present value payment)
2nd to 10th years =   3,420 (present value payment each and every year for 9 years)

Rate of Return   Age 65
Insured: 8.06%
Beneficiary: 14.26%

Life Insurance: Its Rate of Return

How does Brownlie factor in the current cash surrender value in his comparisons?

The current cash surrender value has to be entered as a present value payment for both the existing policy (policies) and the proposed replaced and/or exchanged policy (policies).

What really is the significance of any variance in the rate of return?

Do not dismiss what appears to be only a tiny variance in the rate of return. A 15% rate of return, for example, over a 15-year period does not appear to be appreciably more than a 13% rate of return. But, indeed, a 15% rate of return is significantly more important. It is not simply a 2% difference.

Look at it this way. You go down to your bank and talk to your banker. You tell the banker, "I want to have $100,000 in your bank 15 years from now. I'm going to assume that you will give me 15% compound interest on my money for the next 15 years. Now, please tell me how much money I have to give this bank each and every year."

And the banker's answer is, "You must give this bank $1,827.57 each and every year for the next 15 years. At the end of those 15 years, you will have your $100,000 goal realized."

Now you decide to walk across the street and visit another bank and banker. The second banker listens to you outline your goals and replies, "I can only give you 13% compound interest for the next 15 years. You must give this bank $2,189.54 each and every year for the next 15 years in order to accomplish your goal of $100,000."

Life Insurance: Replaced or Exchanged?

Now, obviously, the difference between what you have to pay one bank and another bank for 15 years is $361.97 each year. Maybe you don't think that a 2% variance in the rate of return is a big one. Try this on! The $361.97 invested each and every year at 5% net interest for 15 years will grow to $8,201.33.

The same analogy holds true for life insurance companies. A policy providing a $100,000 death benefit in 15 years with a 15% rate of return to the beneficiary is obviously a better buy than a policy providing $100,000 death benefit in 15 years with a 13% rate of return to the beneficiary.

6

A DISCUSSION OF LIFE INSURANCE PLANS AND METHODS OF PREMIUM PAYMENT

The reader should keep in mind the fact that a plan of life insurance is *not* the same as a method of premium payment. Some of the life insurance plans are:

- Yearly Renewable Term
- Whole Life (Ordinary Life)
- Adjustable Premium Whole Life (Universal Life)
- Variable Life
- Life Paid-up at Age 65

Life Insurance: Its Rate of Return

- Economatic
- Graded Premium Life
- Group Executive Ordinary

Some of the methods of premium payment are:

- Tax-Qualified Minimum Deposit
- Premium Offset/Vanishing Premium
- Split Dollar
- IRC Section 79
- Retired Lives Reserve
- Keogh Plan Purchase
- Corporate Retirement Plan Purchase
- Deferred Compensation Plan Purchase
- Death Benefit Only Plan Purchase
- IRC Section 501(c)(9) Trust

Note: For a thorough explanation of all life insurance plans and methods of premium payment shown in this book, I strongly suggest that you consult your life insurance agent and/or your life insurance company.

What are the life insurance plans shown in this book?

The life insurance plans shown in this book are:

- Yearly Renewable Term with Reissue Provision[1]
- Yearly Renewable TerM without Reissue Provision
- Whole Life (Ordinary Life)
- Adjustable Premium Whole Life (Universal Life)
- Variable Life

---

[1] Generally with evidence of insurability the policy premiums will be "reissued" with lower premiums for a period of time then provided in the original policy.

Life Insurance Plans and Premium Payment

Why did I choose these insurance plans for this book?

The plans of life insurance shown in this book have been selected by me because I believe there are only two types of life insurance; term life and whole life. Every other type of life insurance is actually a variation of term or whole life.

Whole Life is the traditional level premium plan of life insurance. Two new variations of Whole Life are Adjustable Premium Whole Life (Universal Life) and Variable Life.

What are the methods of premium payment shown in this book?

The methods of premium payment shown in this book are:
- Tax-Qualified Minimum Deposit pursuant to Section 264 of the Internal Revenue Code (generically referred to as "the 4 out of 7 plan"); and
- Premium Offset/Vanishing Premium

Why did I choose these methods of premium payment for this book?

The methods of premium payment shown in this book have been selected by me because they are two of the most popular methods advocated by life insurance agents in the current marketplace.

Does this book advocate any particular life insurance plan or method of premium payment?

No! I do not believe there is any one life insurance plan or method of premium payment suitable for everyone. Choices should be made based upon individual situations.

Life Insurance: Its Rate of Return

What are the sources for the official ledger statements used in this book?

New England Mutual Life Insurance Company and The John Hancock Variable Life Insurance Company were the sources for the official ledger statements used in this book.

Why is 1983 the year to buy Whole Life (Ordinary Life)?

The Tax Equity and Fiscal Responsibility Act of 1982 (referred to by the acronym TEFRA) granted life insurance companies stopgap legislation for only two years. Because the life insurance companies realized tax savings through TEFRA, the companies have elected to pass these savings on to the policyholders by making Whole Life (Ordinary Life) more attractive to purchase. If TEFRA is not extended, the life insurance companies may not be able to offer a whole life product in 1984 as attractively as it can be offered in 1983.

What should you know before you buy Yearly Renewable Term Life insurance?

Before you buy Yearly Renewable Term Life insurance you should know whether or not the life insurance company, from whom you are considering a purchase of term insurance, is reinsuring their term insurance with another life insurance company. If they are, and if the reinsurance company begins to lose money, the following effects could occur:
- Mutual life insurance companies may have to severely reduce the projected dividends on their term life insurance;
- Stock life insurance companies may start to charge premiums at the maximum rate rather than at the current rate.

Life Insurance Plans and Premium Payment

What should the public expect from the life insurance agent?

The public has the absolute right to expect total disclosure from the life insurance agent about all plans of life insurance and all methods of premium payment available. For example, as a life insurance agent I would present to my client the life insurance plans and methods of premium payment available and, in addition, I would carefully discuss direct recognition, new money rate, blended money rate and the interest assumption.

What is meant by "direct recognition"?

Direct recognition applies to all life insurance plans except term insurance. Direct recognition means the life insurance company "directly recognizes" those policyholders who do not borrow on their life insurance policies and those who do borrow on their life insurance policies. The dividends are substantially higher for those policyholders who do not borrow on their life insurance; the dividends are lower for those policyholders who do borrow on their life insurance. There are two points to remember:

(1) In 1983 not all life insurance companies are using direct recognition. Some are, most are not.

(2) You must study the official ledger statement of the life insurance company in order to know whether or not direct recognition is used in the life insurance plan being recommended for your consideration. Look for a statement on the official ledger statement which says something like this: "Illustrated dividends assume no loans on the policy. Policy loans will reduce the dividends." This tells you that direct recognition is being used.

Life Insurance: Its Rate of Return

What is meant by "new money rate", "blended money rate" and "interest assumption"?

New money rate is the earnings on investments placed currently. A portfolio rate is the return on all the investments of the company. A blended money rate is a mixture of new money and portfolio rates. In 1983 new money rates are higher than portfolio rates because of the investments made some years ago. At this point blended money rates would fall between new money and portfolio rates.

Interest assumption is the rate the company credits on the cash values of Universal Life and Excess Interest policies. In most instances, companies use new money rates for these contracts.

7
EXPLANATION OF THE BROWNLIE METHOD OF CALCULATIONS

What is the definition of the word method?

Webster's New Collegiate Dictionary, (1981 edition) defines method as "a systematic procedure, technique, or mode of inquiry employed by or proper to a particular discipline or art; a way, technique, or process of or for doing something."

What is the Brownlie Method of Calculations?

The Brownlie Method of Calculations is a method which uses a Hewlett-Packard 41-C (HP-41-C) Hand Calculator with

Life Insurance: Its Rate of Return

Financial Decisions Module as an integral part of the technique and/or process to arrive at the compound interest return for life insurance and for any other financial transaction.

Can you use any other hand calculator for the Brownlie Method of Calculations?

The Brownlie Method of Calculations can be adapted to any hand calculator which has the financial decisions capability and sufficient memories. However, you must know how to use each hand calculator and which commands to give the calculator. Therefore, you will most likely have to adapt the Brownlie Method of Calculations to the hand calculator you choose to use.

Who created the financial decisions module for the HP-41-C Hand Calculator?

Hewlett-Packard created the financial decisions module for the HP-41-C Hand Calculator.

Do the instruction manuals for the HP-41-C Hand Calculator and Financial Decisions Module mention life insurance?

No! They do not mention life insurance.

If Brownlie did not create the Financial Decisions Module, how can he use the term Brownlie Method of Calculations?

The instruction manuals accompanying the Hewlett-Packard 41-C Hand Calculator and the Financial Decisions Module *do not include* any examples to show how they

Explanation of the Brownlie Method of Calculations

could be used to determine the rate of return for life insurance.

I, Bill Brownlie, figured out on my own, after countless hours of trial and error, how to use the HP-41-C Hand Calculator with Financial Decisions Module in order to determine the rates of return on life insurance. In Chapter 8 I will show you what I learned and the commands I created in order to do what I wanted to do.

Therefore, it is my conviction and contention that the Brownlie Method of Calculations is the only known published method available which shows how to use any hand calculator to determine the rates of return on life insurance.

What did Brownlie contribute to the practical application of the HP-41-C Hand Calculator with Financial Decisions Module in order to arrive at the rate of return for life insurance?

As was stated previously, the instruction manuals do not mention life insurance. Therefore, it became necessary for me to determine exactly what questions to ask the Customer Support Division of Hewlett-Packard in order to know how to use the Financial Decisions Module to solve problems in the areas of life insurance.

Does the Brownlie Method of Calculations make any assumptions?

No, it does not! The Brownlie Method simply takes raw data — if you will, the facts — on present value payment, future value and time span and calculates the rate of return in terms of compound interest. One need not be an adept mathematician in order to do this. But one must know what orders to give the HP-41-C Hand Calculator with Financial Decisions Module, or the hand calculator of your choice.

Life Insurance: Its Rate of Return

Can you give some examples?

Life Insurance
    $100,000 Whole Life (Ordinary Life)
    Male, age 55
    Premium: $3,316.00
    Ledger statement shows:
      Total cash value, 5 years $12,196
      Total death benefit, 5 years $106,379
    Present value payments for 5 years are $3,316 each year.
    Future value to the insured if the policy is surrendered in 5 years: $12,196.00
    Future value to the beneficiary if death occurs in 5 years: $106,379.00
    Insured's rate of return: –10.07%
    Beneficiary's rate of return: 70.04%

Home Purchase
    $100,000 purchase price in 19--
    No mortgage. $100,000 paid in cash.
    Home sold 20 years later for $400,000.

Present value payment:	$100,000
Future value:	$400,000
Time span:	20 yrs.
Rate of Return:	7.18%

Explanation of the Brownlie Method of Calculations

Mutual Fund Investment

$10,000 invested 1978.

Mutual fund appreciated in value during the five year priod (1978-1983) to $33,000.

Present value payment:	$10,000
Future value:	$33,000
Time span:	5 yrs.
Rate of Return:	26.97%

Conversion of Percentage Increases to Compound Interest

450% appreciation over 5 years. What is this in terms of compound interest?

Future value:	450% + 100%	= 550%
Present value:		100%
Time span:		5 years
Rate of return:		40.63%

What do I consider to be the singular appeal of the Brownlie Method of Calculations?

I consider the singular appeal of the Brownlie Method of Calculations to be the ability to do it yourself. You do not need an expensive computer. You do not have to rely on anyone, anyone's word, any company, or any institution. You can do the calculations yourself.

8

RATE OF RETURN FOR LIFE INSURANCE PLANS USING THE BROWNLIE METHOD OF CALCULATIONS

The calculations in this chapter have been done with the following facts in mind:

Fact #1   The future value to the beneficiary (the death benefit) is not subject to Federal Income Tax.

Fact #2   The future value to the insured (the cash value, total cash value, and/or net equity value) has

Life Insurance: Its Rate of Return

been taken directly from the official ledger statement of the life insurance company. Neither the official ledger statement of the life insurance company, nor the author of this book, have taken into consideration whether or not any taxes are due. Taxes are due if, in fact, the insured surrenders the policy and the cash surrender value, total cash value and/or net equity value, exceed the premiums paid. If any tax is due, it would reduce the rate of return to the insured.

Fact #3   Numerous attorneys and accountants have assured me that the predominant tax bracket in the United States today is the 40% tax bracket. This is true for both individual taxpayers and corporate taxpayers.

Rate of Return for Life Insurance Using Brownlie

$100,000 Yearly Renewable Term with Reissue Provision, Male, Age 35

Federal Tax Bracket Assumption:
  40% Individual Taxpayer
  40% Corporate Taxpayer

Time Span	Beneficiary's Rate of Return	Before Tax Rate of Return Necessary to Duplicate the Beneficiary's Rate of Return in Another Financial Product
1 year	57,042.86%	95,071.43%
5 years	227.57%	379.28%
15 years	38.43%	64.06%
30 years	13.33%	22.22%
*45 years	3.15%	5.25%

*Beyond life expectancy

Time Span	Insured's Rate of Return	Before Tax Rate of Return Necessary to Duplicate the Insured's Rate of Return in Another Financial Product
1 year	−100%	NONE
5 years	−100%	NONE
15 years	−100%	NONE
30 years	−100%	NONE
*45 years	−100%	NONE

*Beyond life expectancy

Note: Dividends as declared have been used in reduction of the premium. Dividends are projections into the future based on the current dividend scale of the insurance company. Dividends are not guaranteed.

Life Insurance: Its Rate of Return

$100,000 Yearly Renewable Term without Reissue Provision, Male, Age 35

Federal Tax Bracket Assumption:
 40% Individual Taxpayer
 40% Corporate Taxpayer

Time Span	Beneficiary's Rate of Return	Before Tax Rate of Return Necessary to Duplicate the Beneficiary's Rate of Return in Another Financial Product
1 year	57,042.86%	95,071.43%
5 years	227.34%	378.90%
15 years	37.06%	61.76%
30 years	11.27%	18.78%
*45 years	1.16%	1.93%

*Beyond life expectancy

Time Span	Insured's Rate of Return	Before Tax Rate of Return Necessary to Duplicate the Insured's Rate of Return in Another Financial Product
1 year	–100%	NONE
5 years	–100%	NONE
15 years	–100%	NONE
30 years	–100%	NONE
*45 years	–100%	NONE

*Beyond life expectancy

Note: Dividends as declared have been used in reduction of the premium. Dividends are projections into the future based on the current dividend scale of the insurance company. Dividends are not guaranteed.

Rate of Return for Life Insurance Using Brownlie

$100,000 Whole Life (Ordinary Life), Male, Age 35

Federal Tax Bracket Assumption:
40% Individual Taxpayer
40% Corporate Taxpayer

Time Span	Beneficiary's Rate of Return	Before Tax Rate of Return Necessary to Duplicate the Beneficiary's Rate of Return in Another Financial Product
1 year	7,586.40%	12,643.99%
5 years	112.33%	187.21%
15 years	21.08%	35.13%
30 years	9.19%	15.31%
*45 years	7.14%	11.90%

*Beyond life expectancy

Time Span	Insured's Rate of Return	Before Tax Rate of Return Necessary to Duplicate the Insured's Rate of Return in Another Financial Product
1 year	−100%	NONE
5 years	−5.31%	NONE
15 years	4.95%	8.25%
30 years	6.43%	10.72%
*45 years	6.65%	11.08%

*Beyond life expectancy

Note: Dividends as declared have been used in reduction of the premium. From the 18th year on, the projected declared dividend is in excess of the premium of $1,301.00. Dividends are projections into the future based on the current dividend scale of the insurance company. Dividends are not guaranteed.

Life Insurance: Its Rate of Return

$100,000 Adjustable Premium Whole Life (Universal Life), Male, Age 35

Federal Tax Bracket Assumption:
40% Individual Taxpayer
40% Corporate Taxpayer

Time Span	Beneficiary's Rate of Return is Predicated on the Universal Life Interest Assumption of 10%, if Realized	Before Tax Rate of Return Necessary to Duplicate the Beneficiary's Rate of Return in Another Financial Product
1 year	9,820.63%	16,367.72%
5 years	123.55%	205.91%
15 years	21.50%	35.83%
30 years	6.90%	11.50%
*45 years	3.14%	5.23%

*Beyond life expectancy

Time Span	Insured's Rate of Return is Predicated on the Universal Life Interest Assumption of 10%, if Realized	Before Tax Rate of Return Necessary to Duplicate the Insured's Rate of Return in Another Financial Product
1 year	−96.53%	NONE
5 years	−9.14%	NONE
15 years	4.46%	7.43%
30 years	7.51%	12.52%
*45 years	8.45%	14.08%

*Beyond life expectancy

Note: This is an Option A Universal Life rate of return calculation. Option A means a level death benefit which never exceeds $100,000. The premium of $1,008.00 is the present value payment each and every year.

Rate of Return for Life Insurance Using Brownlie

$100,000 Adjustable Premium Whole Life (Universal Life), Male, Age 35

Federal Tax Bracket Assumption:
40% Individual Taxpayer
40% Corporate Taxpayer

Time Span	Beneficiary's Rate of Return is Predicated on the Universal Life Interest Assumption of 10%, if Realized	Before Tax Rate of Return Necessary to Duplicate the Beneficiary's Rate of Return in Another Financial Product
1 year	9,823.51%	16,372.52%
5 years	125.50%	209.17%
15 years	23.58%	39.31%
30 years	10.42%	17.37%
*45 years	8.27%	13.79%

*Beyond life expectancy

Time Span	Insured's Rate of Return is Predicated on the Universal Life Interest Assumption of 10%, if Realized	Before Tax Rate of Return Necessary to Duplicate the Insured's Rate of Return in Another Financial Product
1 year	−96.63%	NONE
5 years	−9.31%	NONE
15 years	4.15%	6.91%
30 years	6.81%	11.35%
*45 years	7.49%	12.48%

*Beyond life expectancy

Note: This is an Option B Universal Life rate of return calculation. Option B means the death benefit of $100,000 is increased by the cash value. The premium of $1,008.00 is the present value payment each and every year.

Life Insurance: Its Rate of Return

$100,000 Variable Life, Male, Age 35

Federal Tax Bracket Assumption:
40% Individual Taxpayer
40% Corporate Taxpayer

Time Span	Beneficiary's Rate of Return is Predicated on the Variable Life Interest Assumption of 12%, if Realized	Before Tax Rate of Return Necessary to Duplicate the Beneficiary's Rate of Return in Another Financial Product
1 year	6,096.51%	10,160.85%
5 years	106.10%	176.83%
15 years	22.20%	37.00%
30 years	11.22%	18.71%
35 years	10.18%	16.97%
*45 years	The 45th year is not shown on the official ledger statement.	

*Beyond Life Expectancy

Time Span	Insured's Rate of Return is Predicated on the Variable Life Interest Assumption of 12%, if Realized	Before Tax Rate of Return Necessary to Duplicate the Insured's Rate of Return in Another Financial Product
1 year	−58.22%	NONE
5 years	−4.57%	NONE
15 years	5.69%	9.48%
30 years	7.83%	13.05%
35 years	8.03%	13.38%
*45 years	The 45th year is not shown on the official ledger statement.	

*Beyond life expectancy

Note: The projected interest assumption of 12% is not guaranteed. The actual compound interest return is solely dependent on the actual investment performance of the portfolio.

9

RATE OF RETURN FOR METHODS OF PREMIUM PAYMENT USING THE BROWNLIE METHOD OF CALCULATIONS

The calculations in this chapter have been done with the following facts in mind:

Fact #1   The future value to the beneficiary (the death benefit) is not subject to Federal Income Tax.

Fact #2   The future value to the insured (the cash value, total cash value, and/or net equity value)

Life Insurance: Its Rate of Return

has been taken directly from the official ledger statement of the life insurance company. Neither the official ledger statement of the life insurance company, nor the author of this book, have taken into consideration whether or not any taxes are due. Taxes are due if, in fact, the insured surrenders the policy and the cash surrender value, total cash value and/or net equity value, exceeds the premiums paid. If any tax is due, it would reduce the rate of return to the insured.

Fact #3 Numerous attorneys and accountants have assured me that the predominant tax bracket in the United States today is the 40% tax bracket. This is true for both individual taxpayers and corporate taxpayers. However, I strongly believe that only 50% bracket taxpayers should use Tax-Qualified Minimum Deposit as a method of premium payment. You will please note that I have used the 50% tax bracket for my calculations on Tax-Qualified Minimum Deposit examples.

Rate of Return for Premium Payment Using Brownlie

$100,000 Whole Life (Ordinary Life)
Method of Premium Payment, Male, Age 35

Tax-Qualified Minimum Deposit
(Direct Recognition Basis Used)

Federal Tax Bracket Assumption:
50% Individual Taxpayer
50% Corporate Taxpayer

Time Span	Beneficiary's Rate of Return	Before Tax Rate of Return Necessary to Duplicate the Beneficiary's Rate of Return in Another Financial Product
1 year	7,586.40%	15,172.79%
5 years	122.44%	244.87%
15 years	28.80%	57.60%
30 years	13.87%	27.74%
*45 years	The 45th year is not shown on the official ledger statement.	

*Beyond life expectancy

Time Span	Insured's Rate of Return	Before Tax Rate of Return Necessary to Duplicate the Insured's Rate of Return in Another Financial Product
1 year	−100%	NONE
5 years	−12.42%	NONE
15 years	0.72%	1.44%
30 years	0.74%	1.48%
*45 years	The 45th year is not shown on the official ledger statement.	

*Beyond life expectancy

Life Insurance: Its Rate of Return

Note: It is my opinion that only 50% tax bracket taxpayers should consider Tax-Qualified Minimum Deposit as a method of premium payment for life insurance. Dividends as declared have been used to purchase one year of term insurance equal to the cash value; the balance has been used to reduce the premium. Dividends are projections into the future based on the current dividend scale of the insurance company. Dividends are not guaranteed. Dividends are on a direct recognition basis.

Rate of Return for Premium Payment Using Brownlie

$100,000 Whole Life (Ordinary Life) Method of Premium Payment, Male, Age 35

Tax-Qualified Minimum Deposit
(Direct Recognition Basis Not Used)

Federal Tax Bracket Assumption:
50% Individual Taxpayer
50% Corporate Taxpayer

Time Span	Beneficiary's Rate of Return	Before Tax Rate of Return Necessary to Duplicate the Beneficiary's Rate of Return in Another Financial Product
1 year	6,221.11%	12,442.23%
5 years	113.53%	227.05%
15 years	27.65%	55.29%
30 years	14.78%	29.55%
*45 years	The 45th year is not shown on the official ledger statement.	

*Beyond life expectancy

Time Span	Insured's Rate of Return	Before Tax Rate of Return Necessary to Duplicate the Insured's Rate of Return in Another Financial Product
1 year	−100%	NONE
5 years	−22.75%	NONE
15 years	4.11%	8.23%
30 years	9.15%	18.30%
*45 years	The 45th year is not shown on the official ledger statement.	

*Beyond life expectancy

Note: It is my opinion that only 50% tax bracket taxpayers should consider Tax-Qualified Minimum Deposit as a method of premium payment for life insurance. Dividends as declared have been used to purchase one year of term insurance equal to the cash value; the balance has been used to reduce the premium. Dividends are projections into the future based on the current dividend scale of the insurance company. Dividends are not guaranteed. Dividends are not on a direct recognition basis.

Rate of Return for Premium Payment Using Brownlie

$100,000 Whole Life (Ordinary Life)
Method of Premium Payment, Male, Age 35

Premium Offset/Vanishing Premium

Federal Tax Bracket Assumption:
40% Individual Taxpayer
40% Corporate Taxpayer

Time Span	Beneficiary's Rate of Return	Before Tax Rate of Return Necessary to Duplicate the Beneficiary's Rate of Return in Another Financial Product
1 year	7,586.40%	12,643.55%
5 years	112.05%	186.75%
15 years	20.65%	34.42%
30 years	9.71%	16.19%
*45 years	7.82%	13.03%

*Beyond life expectancy

Time Span	Insured's Rate of Return	Before Tax Rate of Return Necessary to Duplicate the Insured's Rate of Return in Another Financial Product
1 year	–100%	NONE
5 years	–4.60%	NONE
15 years	5.39%	8.98%
30 years	6.64%	11.07%
*45 years	6.95%	11.59%

*Beyond life expectancy

Note: The dividends as declared are used to purchase additional paid-up life insurance. The full premium of

Life Insurance: Its Rate of Return

$1,301.00 is to be paid each and every year for nine years. Starting in the 10th year, the newly declared dividend is used to reduce the premium. Any balance due is paid from the dividends that were built-up during the first nine years. From the 10th year on, a combination of the newly declared dividend and previously built-up dividends pay the premium. Dividends are projections into the future based on the current dividend scale of the insurance company. Dividends are not guaranteed.

10

INTRODUCTION TO THE HEWLETT-PACKARD 41-C HAND CALCULATOR WITH FINANCIAL DECISIONS MODULE

Before I introduce you to the Hewlett-Packard 41-C Hand Calculator with Financial Decisions Module, I would like to make certain points as clear as possible.

- Through trial and error involving countless hours of personal discipline, I taught myself how to use the HP-41-C Hand Calculator with Financial Decisions Module in order to be able to calculate the rate of return on life insurance. There is no question in my mind that I am now an expert on using the HP-41-C

Life Insurance: Its Rate of Return

Hand Calculator and its Financial Decisions Module (FDM) for that specific purpose.

- The HP-41-C does not perform financial decisions calculations. You must purchase, as I did, the Financial Decisions Module (FDM) on a separate basis. The FDM is accompanied by an overlay index card and instructions for the use and placement of its overlay index card.
- I am not an expert in the engineering intricacies or the total capability of the HP-41-C Hand Calculator with FDM.
- If, after reading this book, you have any questions regarding the HP-41-C with FDM, I respectfully suggest that you do what I had to do ... call the Hewlett-Packard Corporation (Telephone: 503/757-2000) and ask for the Customer Support Division.
- I have used the HP-41-C with FDM because I determined that it best filled my needs. It is essential that you have a hand calculator which is able to accomodate enough memories to handle all the calculations you wish to do. In order for me to do all the calculations shown in this book, it was necessary for me to buy and insert into the calculator a separate memory module which provided an additional 63 memories, giving me a total of 126 memories.
- It is important for you to realize that for my purposes I have disregarded the Hewlett-Packard "MONEY" and "IRR" buttons which appear on the FDM overlay index card. This is a prime example of how I modified the use of the calculator to suit my purposes.
- You do not have to be an adept mathematician to use this calculator, nor do you have to be an adept mathematician to use and understand the Brownlie Method of Calculations for the rate of return on life insurance.

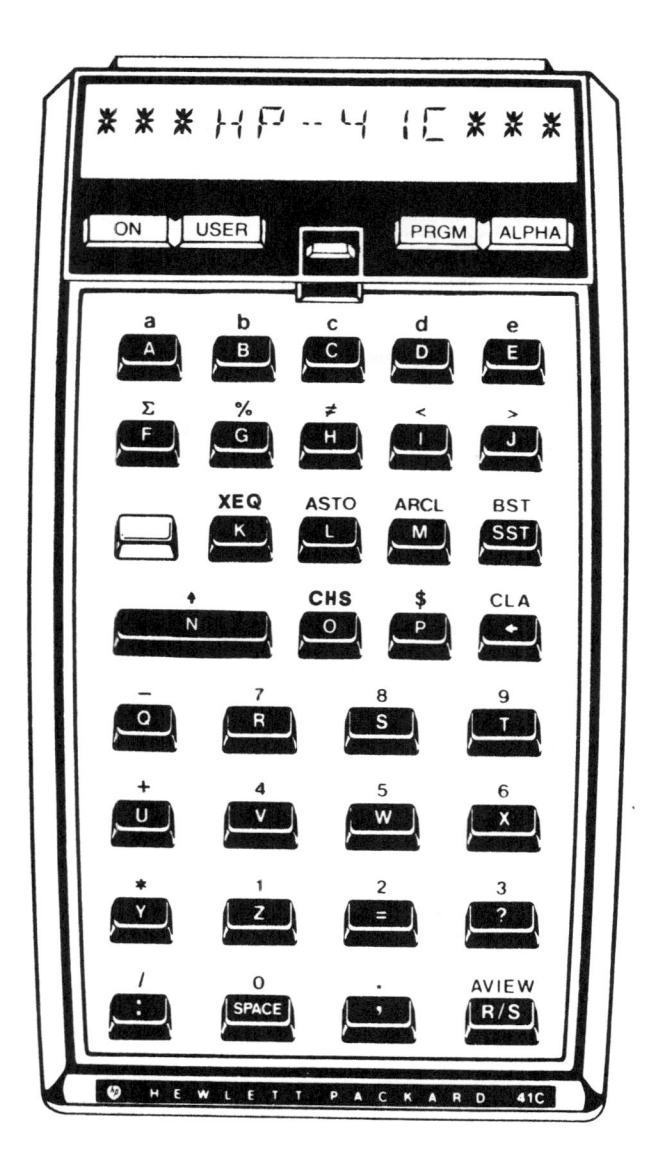

Introduction to Hewlett-Packard 41-C Calculator

Hewlett-Packard 41C Hand Calculator

Life Insurance: Its Rate of Return

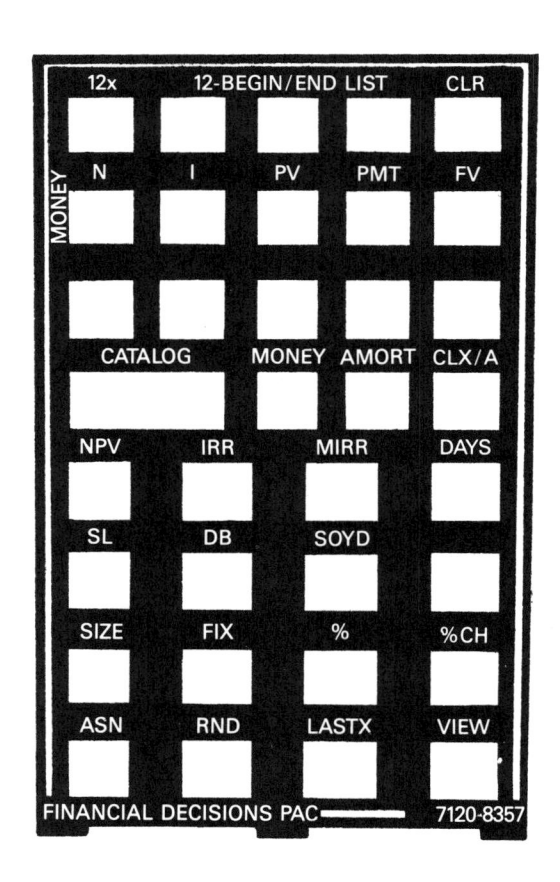

Financial Decisions Module

Introduction to Hewlett-Packard 41-C Calculator

The Hewlett-Packard 41-C Hand Calculator with Financial Decisions Module

(1) ON

Turn the calculator "ON" by pressing the button.

(2) XEQ

Before you do anything, you have to tell the calculator to execute that which you wish to do. Therefore, press the button marked "XEQ" which means to execute a command.

(3) ALPHA

After you have decided to execute a command, you must enter the *size* of the particular program you are going to execute. The only way you may enter letters into the calculator (the small blue letters) is by first pressing the button marked "ALPHA". Conversely, if you wish to add numbers into the calculator, you must press "ALPHA" in order to remove the ALPHA execution from the calculator.

(4) SIZE

Completely disregard the word "SIZE" that is already in place on the FDM overlay index card. You must always enter SIZE manually by pressing the individual blue letters spelling out the word "S-I-Z-E". Also, please remember that for all calculations, you will use either the MONEY program or the IRR program. Both the MONEY program and the IRR program will be explained later in this chapter.

Both the MONEY program and the IRR program have a SIZE. The word "SIZE" is entered as I have explained above. After you enter SIZE, you must press the ALPHA button again. Enter the individual numbers for

Life Insurance: Its Rate of Return

the SIZE of the program you are calculating. The minimum SIZE for the MONEY program is *always* 015. Use the MONEY program when you are paying the same present value payment (premium) for the number of years you are measuring. Use the IRR program when the present value payments (premiums) are not the same every year.

The amounts of the individual present value payments (premiums) change each and every year. The IRR program refers to these present value payments as the "CASH FLOWS" and uses the symbol "CFS." The SIZE for the IRR program is determined by the following formula:

SIZE for IRR program equals the number of cash flows plus 17. Or, written another way,
SIZE for IRR = Number of CFS + 17.

The number of cash flows (CFS) is always one (1) more than the number of present value payments paid. This is because the one additional cash flow always represents either the death benefit (if you are measuring the beneficiary's rate of return), or the cash value, total cash value and/or net equity value (if you are measuring the insured's rate of return).

There are two ways to enter the present value payment (premium) for the IRR program. When you know the present value payment is going to be different each and every year, you must enter the present value payment year by year. If the present value payment is going to remain the same for a certain number of years and then change for a certain number of years, you may enter the present value payment as "GROUPS". The size for GROUPS in the IRR program is the number of GROUPS times (x) 2 + 17.

Introduction to Hewlett-Packard 41-C Calculator

EXAMPLES:

MONEY program SIZE example is always 015.
IRR program SIZE example:

(A). Present value payments (premiums) for ten (10) years:

Time Span	Present Value Payments
1	100
2	105
3	110
4	115
5	120
6	125
7	130
8	135
9	140
10	145
11	50,000

This represents CASH FLOW 11 (CF 11) which is the 10th year death benefit.

Total cash flows is 11.
SIZE is the number of cash flows plus (+) 17.
Therefore, SIZE equals 028.   SIZE = 028

(B). Present value payments (premiums) for years 1 to 5 is $85.00 each and every year.
Present value payments (premiums) for years 6 to 10 is $115.00 each and every year.
The 10th year death benefit is $50,000.

Based on the figures above, we can use three (3) groups.

```
GROUP 1   CF AMT = ?   85      (CF AMT means
No. CFS        5                cash flow amount)
GROUP 2   CF AMT = ?   115
No. CFS        5
GROUP 3   CF AMT = ?   50,000
No. CFS        1
```

SIZE for GROUPS is always the number of GROUPS times (x) 2 + 17.
Therefore, SIZE equals 023.   SIZE = 023

Life Insurance: Its Rate of Return

(5) Number of programs to be used
For all calculations, you will use only one (1) of two (2) programs:
   MONEY program *or* IRR program

(6) MONEY Program
Note: Please disregard the word "MONEY" which is already in place on the Financial Decisions Module overlay index card. You must always enter the word MONEY manually by pressing the individual blue letters spelling out the word "M-O-N-E-Y".

Now give the following commands to the calculator for the MONEY program in the order shown:

ON — XEQ — ALPHA — SIZE (S-I-Z-E) — ALPHA — 015

XEQ — ALPHA — MONEY (M-O-N-E-Y) — ALPHA

CLR ?   R/S   (The calculator is now asking, "Are you clear as to what you wish to do?" Say "YES" by pressing the button marked R/S.)

END ? N R/S

BEGIN   READY

The entire MONEY program sequence is on the top row of the Financial Decisions Module overlay index card, reading from left to right:

- **N** stands for time span. If you are measuring for ten (10) years, you would enter the number ten (10) then press N.

- **I** stands for interest. When you wish to solve for interest, "I" in the MONEY program always equals the rate of return; press I.

84

Introduction to Hewlett-Packard 41-C Calculator

PV stands for present value.

PMT stands for payment. In the MONEY program when you are entering the premium, you will always enter first the dollar amount of the premium, then CHS (CHS will be explained later in the chapter), and then PMT.

FV stands for future value. Depending upon which future value you are entering (either the dollar amount representing the death benefit, or the dollar amount representing the cash value, total cash value and/or net equity value), you enter the particular dollar amount, then press FV.

Example: This calculation is for a 10-year (10) measurement with a 10th year death benefit of $100,000 and present value payments (premiums) paid of $200 each and every year.

ON — XEQ — ALPHA — SIZE (S-I-Z-E) — ALPHA — 015

XEQ — ALPHA — MONEY (M-O-N-E-Y) — ALPHA

CLR ? R/S

END ? N R/S

BEGIN READY

    100,000   FV
       200   CHS PMT
        10   N
         I
         I = Now calculating.
         I = 70.51%
         I = Rate of Return

Life Insurance: Its Rate of Return

(7) IRR Program
Note: Please disregard the word "IRR" which is already in place on the Financial Decisions Module overlay index card. You must always enter the word IRR manually by pressing the individual blue letters spelling out the word "I-R-R".

Now give the following commands to the calculator for the IRR program in the order shown:

ON — XEQ — ALPHA — SIZE (S-I-Z-E) — ALPHA — 023
(number of cash flows is 6 + 17 = 023)

XEQ — ALPHA — IRR (I-R-R) — ALPHA

CLR ? The calculator is now asking, "Are you clear as to what you wish to do?"
Say "YES" by pressing the button marked R/S.

GROUPS ? The calculator is now asking, "Are you going to use GROUPS?"
In this introductory exercise GROUPS are not being used so the answer is "NO".
"NO" is entered by pressing the button marked with the blue letter "N", the word "ENTER" above it, and an arrow pointing upward.
Press the button marked N.
Now you want to tell the calculator to proceed. Do so by saying "YES". Press the button marked R/S.

TOTAL CFS = ? The calculator is now asking, "How many cash flows are to be utilized in this calculation?" There are six (6) cash flows. Five (5) present value payments plus (+) the 5th year death benefit.
Tell the calculator to proceed by entering the number "6". Then, press the button marked R/S.

86

Introduction to Hewlett-Packard 41-C Calculator

CF 1 CF AMT = ? The calculator is now asking, "What is the dollar amount of cash flow (CF) 1?" In this exercise, the present value payments (premiums) are:

1st year: $200.00
2nd year: $205.00
3rd year: $210.00
4th year: $215.00
5th year: $220.00

The 5th year death benefit is $100,000 which will be cash flow (CF) 6.

Now, for CF 1 CF AMT=?, answer:

CF 1 CF AMT = ?	200	CHS	R/S
CF 2 CF AMT = ?	205	CHS	R/S
CF 3 CF AMT = ?	210	CHS	R/S
CF 4 CF AMT = ?	215	CHS	R/S
CF 5 CF AMT = ?	220	CHS	R/S
CF 6 CF AMT = ?	100,000		R/S

Note: Any time you are entering a benefit that is to be *received* (either the death benefit or the cash value, total cash value/net equity value), you *never* enter "CHS" after the dollar amount.

CF CHANGES ? The calculator is now asking, "Are there any cash flow (CF) changes?" The answer is "NO". Press the button marked with the blue letter "N", the word "Enter" above it, and an arrow pointing upward.

Tell the calculator to proceed by pressing the button marked R/S.

The calculator is now figuring the rate of return. You will see little symbols which look like little "birds" flying across your display. It will take a few moments (perhaps even a few minutes) to complete the calculation.

IRR = 221.14%   IRR = Rate of Return

Life Insurance: Its Rate of Return

(8) Symbol for NO
The symbol for "NO" is the button marked with the blue letter "N" and the word "ENTER" above it with an arrow pointing upward.

(9) Symbol for YES
The symbol for "YES" is the button marked "R/S". When you wish to answer "YES", press the button marked "R/S".

(10) Symbol for Negative Cost Entry
The entry "CHS" is used both in the MONEY program and the IRR program. This is always a negative entry meaning it represents a cost *not* a benefit to be received. Therefore, when you press the CHS button the number you entered will appear on the display as a negative number. On the official ledger statements you will see columns of figures which you will know are present value payments (premiums). Whenever you see a minus sign (-) following the amounts in those columns, never use CHS in your calculations. Where you see zero (0) in those columns, never use CHS in your calculations.

(11) Procedure for Clearing the Display
In order to clear the display, press the amber colored button *and* the button marked with the arrow pointing to the left.

(12) Procedure for Correcting Entry Figure Error
If you should inadvertently enter "149", for example, instead of "148", you may correct the wrong digit by pressing the button with the arrow pointing to the left. Using this button allows you to correct your entry, digit by digit, beginning with the last digit entered.

Introduction to Hewlett-Packard 41-C Calculator

(13) What does "CLR?" mean?

The symbol "CLR?" will appear in the display for both MONEY and IRR programs. When this symbol appears, the calculator is asking, "Are you clear about what you are asking the calculator to do?" Tell the calculator to proceed by answering "YES". The symbol for YES has been explained above.

(14) What does "END" mean?

This question appears in the display for the MONEY program. When this question appears, you will answer "NO". The symbol for NO has been explained above.

After you answer NO, tell the calculator to proceed by pressing the button marked R/S.

At this point the word "BEGIN" will appear on the display.

Almost immediately the word BEGIN will disappear, and the word "READY" will appear on the display.

When the word READY appears on the display, you will be ready to enter your MONEY program calculations.

Note: END means end of year; BEGIN means beginning of year. The author bases all of his calculations on the beginning of the year.

11

HOW TO CALCULATE THE RATE OF RETURN FOR LIFE INSURANCE PLANS

Life Insurance: Its Rate of Return

HOW TO CALCULATE THE BENEFICIARY'S RATE OF RETURN FOR YEARLY RENEWABLE TERM WITH REISSUE PROVISION

Here is a series of unequal present value payments (premiums) which change each and every year. Future value (the death benefit) is always the same. The time span is the number of years you wish to measure.

Program = IRR

One (1) Year Measurement

ON — XEQ — ALPHA — SIZE — ALPHA — 019
XEQ — ALPHA — IRR — ALPHA
CLR ?   R/S
GROUPS ?   N   R/S
TOTL CFS = ?   2   R/S

| CF 1 | CF AMT = ? | 175 | CHS | R/S |
| CF 2 | CF AMT = ? | 100,000 | | R/S |

CF CHANGES ?   N   R/S

Now calculating — will take a few minutes.

IRR = 57,042.86%   IRR = Rate of Return

CF 2 is the 1st-year death benefit.

CLEAR DISPLAY. You must reenter program.

Calculate the Rate of Return for Life Insurance

Five (5) Year Measurement

ON — XEQ — ALPHA — SIZE — ALPHA — 023
XEQ — ALPHA — IRR — ALPHA
CLR ?   R/S
GROUPS ?   N   R/S
TOTL CFS = ?   6   R/S

CF 1	CF AMT = ?	175	CHS	R/S
CF 2	CF AMT = ?	198	CHS	R/S
CF 3	CF AMT = ?	224	CHS	R/S
CF 4	CF AMT = ?	253	CHS	R/S
CF 5	CF AMT = ?	188	CHS	R/S
CF 6	CF AMT = ?	100,000		R/S

CF CHANGES?   N   R/S

Now calculating — will take a few minutes.

IRR = 227.57%   IRR = Rate of Return

CF 6 is the 5th-year death benefit.

CLEAR DISPLAY. You must reenter the program.

Life Insurance: Its Rate of Return

Fifteen (15) Year Management

ON — XEQ — ALPHA — SIZE — ALPHA — 033
XEQ — ALPHA — IRR — ALPHA
CLR ?   R/S
GROUPS ?   N   R/S
TOTL CFS = ?   16   R/S

CF 1	CF AMT = ?	175	CHS	R/S
CF 2	CF AMT = ?	198	CHS	R/S
CF 3	CF AMT = ?	224	CHS	R/S
CF 4	CF AMT = ?	253	CHS	R/S
CF 5	CF AMT = ?	188	CHS	R/S
CF 6	CF AMT = ?	222	CHS	R/S
CF 7	CF AMT = ?	262	CHS	R/S
CF 8	CF AMT = ?	310	CHS	R/S
CF 9	CF AMT = ?	210	CHS	R/S
CF 10	CF AMT = ?	260	CHS	R/S
CF 11	CF AMT = ?	321	CHS	R/S
CF 12	CF AMT = ?	394	CHS	R/S
CF 13	CF AMT = ?	251	CHS	R/S
CF 14	CF AMT = ?	313	CHS	R/S
CF 15	CF AMT = ?	398	CHS	R/S
CF 16	CF AMT = ?	100,000		R/S

CF CHANGES ?   N   R/S

Now calculating — will take a few minutes.

IRR = 38.43%   IRR = Rate of Return

CF 16 is the 15th-year death benefit.

CLEAR DISPLAY. You must reenter the program.

Calculate the Rate of Return for Life Insurance

Thirty (30) Year Measurement

ON — XEQ — ALPHA — SIZE — ALPHA — 048
XEQ — ALPHA — IRR — ALPHA
CLR ?   R/S
GROUP ?   N   R/S
TOTL CFS = ?   31   R/S

CF 1	CF AMT = ?	175	CHS	R/S
CF 2	CF AMT = ?	198	CHS	R/S
CF 3	CF AMT = ?	224	CHS	R/S
CF 4	CF AMT = ?	253	CHS	R/S
CF 5	CF AMT = ?	188	CHS	R/S
CF 6	CF AMT = ?	222	CHS	R/S
CF 7	CF AMT = ?	262	CHS	R/S
CF 8	CF AMT = ?	310	CHS	R/S
CF 9	CF AMT = ?	210	CHS	R/S
CF 10	CF AMT = ?	260	CHS	R/S
CF 11	CF AMT = ?	321	CHS	R/S
CF 12	CF AMT = ?	394	CHS	R/S
CF 13	CF AMT = ?	251	CHS	R/S
CF 14	CF AMT = ?	313	CHS	R/S
CF 15	CF AMT = ?	398	CHS	R/S
CF 16	CF AMT = ?	503	CHS	R/S
CF 17	CF AMT = ?	322	CHS	R/S
CF 18	CF AMT = ?	389	CHS	R/S
CF 19	CF AMT = ?	502	CHS	R/S
CF 20	CF AMT = ?	647	CHS	R/S
CF 21	CF AMT = ?	425	CHS	R/S
CF 22	CF AMT = ?	500	CHS	R/S
CF 23	CF AMT = ?	650	CHS	R/S
CF 24	CF AMT = ?	850	CHS	R/S
CF 25	CF AMT = ?	582	CHS	R/S
CF 26	CF AMT = ?	669	CHS	R/S
CF 27	CF AMT = ?	842	CHS	R/S
CF 28	CF AMT = ?	1,120	CHS	R/S
CF 29	CF AMT = ?	840	CHS	R/S
CF 30	CF AMT = ?	957	CHS	R/S
CF 31	CF AMT = ?	100,000		R/S

CF CHANGES ?   N   R/S

Now calculating — will take a few minutes.

IRR = 13.33%   IRR = Rate of Return

CF 31 is the 30th-year death benefit.

CLEAR DISPLAY. You must reenter the program.

Life Insurance: Its Rate of Return

Forty-five (45) Year Measurement

ON — XEQ — ALPHA — SIZE — ALPHA — 063
XEQ — ALPHA — IRR — ALPHA
CLR ? R/S
GROUPS ? N R/S
TOTL CFS = ? 46 R/S

CF 1	CF AMT = ?	175	CHS	R/S
CF 2	CF AMT = ?	198	CHS	R/S
CF 3	CF AMT = ?	224	CHS	R/S
CF 4	CF AMT = ?	253	CHS	R/S
CF 5	CF AMT = ?	188	CHS	R/S
CF 6	CF AMT = ?	222	CHS	R/S
CF 7	CF AMT = ?	262	CHS	R/S
CF 8	CF AMT = ?	310	CHS	R/S
CF 9	CF AMT = ?	210	CHS	R/S
CF 10	CF AMT = ?	260	CHS	R/S
CF 11	CF AMT = ?	321	CHS	R/S
CF 12	CF AMT = ?	394	CHS	R/S
CF 13	CF AMT = ?	251	CHS	R/S
CF 14	CF AMT = ?	313	CHS	R/S
CF 15	CF AMT = ?	398	CHS	R/S
CF 16	CF AMT = ?	503	CHS	R/S
CF 17	CF AMT = ?	322	CHS	R/S
CF 18	CF AMT = ?	389	CHS	R/S
CF 19	CF AMT = ?	502	CHS	R/S
CF 20	CF AMT = ?	647	CHS	R/S
CF 21	CF AMT = ?	425	CHS	R/S
CF 22	CF AMT = ?	500	CHS	R/S
CF 23	CF AMT = ?	650	CHS	R/S
CF 24	CF AMT = ?	850	CHS	R/S
CF 25	CF AMT = ?	582	CHS	R/S
CF 26	CF AMT = ?	669	CHS	R/S
CF 27	CF AMT = ?	842	CHS	R/S
CF 28	CF AMT = ?	1,120	CHS	R/S
CF 29	CF AMT = ?	840	CHS	R/S
CF 30	CF AMT = ?	957	CHS	R/S
CF 31	CF AMT = ?	1,170	CHS	R/S
CF 32	CF AMT = ?	1,564	CHS	R/S
CF 33	CF AMT = ?	1,233	CHS	R/S
CF 34	CF AMT = ?	1,359	CHS	R/S
CF 35	CF AMT = ?	1,595	CHS	R/S
CF 36	CF AMT = ?	2,109	CHS	R/S
CF 37	CF AMT = ?	3,629	CHS	R/S
CF 38	CF AMT = ?	4,012	CHS	R/S
CF 39	CF AMT = ?	4,414	CHS	R/S

Calculate the Rate of Return for Life Insurance

CF 40	CF AMT = ?	4,829	CHS	R/S
CF 41	CF AMT = ?	5,260	CHS	R/S
CF 42	CF AMT = ?	5,610	CHS	R/S
CF 43	CF AMT = ?	6,056	CHS	R/S
CF 44	CF AMT = ?	6,561	CHS	R/S
CF 45	CF AMT = ?	7,114	CHS	R/S
CF 46	CF AMT = ?	100,000		R/S

CF CHANGES ?   N   R/S

Now calculating — will take a few minutes.

IRR = 3.15%   IRR = Rate of Return

CF 46 is the 45th-year death benefit.

CLEAR DISPLAY.

HOW TO CALCULATE THE INSURED'S RATE OF RETURN FOR YEARLY RENEWABLE TERM WITH REISSUE PROVISION

It is not necessary to calculate the insured's rate of return for Yearly Renewable Term with Reissue Provision. There is no future value to the insured. Therefore, the insured's rate of return is always –100% compound.

Life Insurance: Its Rate of Return

LEVEL TERM LEDGER STATEMENT

Plan: YEARLY RENEWABLE TERM TO 100+
Issue Age: 35 Male
Class: PREFERRED STANDARD

Face Amount: $100,000

Policy Year	Annual Premium*	Dividend End of Prior Year**	Net Annual Premium**	Reissue Premiums† 1	Reissue Premiums† 2	Reissue Premiums† 3	Reissue Premiums† 4
1	175	0	175				
2	198	0	198				
3	224	0	224				
4	253	0	253				
5	285	0	285	188			
6	340	33	307	222			
7	364	36	328	262			
8	390	39	351	310			
9	419	43	376	360	210		
10	451	47	404		260		
11	485	51	434		321		
12	523	56	467		394		
13	566	61	505		471	251	
14	612	67	545			313	
15	664	74	590			398	
16	721	81	640			503	
17	785	86	699			623	322
18	855	100	755				389
19	932	116	816				502
20	1017	133	884				647
21							833

Calculate the Rate of Return for Life Insurance

Policy Year	Annual Premium*	Dividend End of Prior Year**	Net Annual Premium**	Reissue Premiums† 5	Reissue Premiums† 6	Reissue Premiums† 7	Reissue Premiums† 8
21	1109	151	958	425			
22	1209	171	1038	500			
23	1316	193	1123	650			
24	1431	217	1214	850			
25	1559	242	1317	1125	582		
26	1704	270	1434		669		
27	1872	302	1570		842		
28	2068	390	1678		1120		
29	2294	459	1835		1537	840	
30	2548	539	2009			957	
31	2823	629	2194			1170	
32	3115	726	2389			1564	
33	3418	830	2588			2168	1233
34	3729	937	2792				1359
35	4054	1047	3007				1595
36	4402	1162	3240				2109
37	4914	1285	3629				3007
38	5479	1467	4012				
39	6081	1667	4414				
40	6709	1880	4829				
41	7362	2102	5260				
42	7943	2333	5610				
43	8595	2539	6056				
44	9331	2770	6561				
45	10144	3030	7114				

Life Insurance: Its Rate of Return

Summary #	Total Annual Premiums+	Total Annual Dividends**	Total Net Premiums**	Total Reissue Premiums†
10 Years	3099	249	2850	2302
15 Years	5949	588	5361	3979
20 Years	10259	1174	9085	6342
Age 60	16883	2267	14616	9349
Age 65	27369	4586	22783	13777
Age 70	44508	9288	35220	20698

Interest-Adjusted Indexes** based on a 5.00% interest rate, for basic policy only: Without Reissue

Life Insurance Net Payment Cost Index	10 yrs: $ 2.76 20 yrs: $ 4.02	Age 65: $ 5.80
Life Insurance Surrender Cost Index	10 yrs: $ 2.76 20 yrs: $ 4.02	Age 65: $ 5.80
Equivalent Level Annual Dividend	10 yrs: $ 0.21 20 yrs: $ 0.45	Age 65: $ 0.95

* Plan renews automatically each year on payment of a renewal premium, but not beyond insured's age 100. Convertible to any Life or Endowment policy with a level face amount prior to the insured's age 70.

† If satisfactory evidence of insurability is submitted at the end of each 4 year period, but not beyond age 69, the lower premium rates will apply. Otherwise, the original rates apply.

** Includes dividend values. Dividends are a return of part of the premium and primarily depend on investment earnings, mortality and expense experience. Dividends are computed on the 1983 dividend scale and are neither guarantees nor estimates for the future.

\# Summary values are calculated as of the end of the year, and due to rounding, may differ slightly from values shown on the ledger page.

\+ Issuance of this plan for the values shown is subject to underwriting approval.

New England Mutual Life Insurance Company

Calculate the Rate of Return for Life Insurance

HOW TO CALCULATE THE BENEFICIARY'S RATE OF RETURN FOR YEARLY RENEWABLE TERM WITHOUT REISSUE PROVISION

Here is a series of unequal present value payments (premiums) which change each and every year. Future value (the death benefit) is always the same. The time span is the number of years you wish to measure.

Program: IRR

One (1) Year Measurement

ON — XEQ — ALPHA — SIZE — ALPHA — 019
XEQ — ALPHA — IRR — ALPHA
CLR ?   R/S
GROUPS ?   N   R/S
TOTL CFS = ?   2   R/S

| CF 1 | CF AMT = ? | 175 | CHS | R/S |
| CF 2 | CF AMT = ? | 100,000 | | R/S |

CF CHANGES ?   N   R/S

Now calculating — will take a few minutes.

IRR = 57,042.86%   IRR = Rate of Return

CF 2 is the 1st-year death benefit.

CLEAR DISPLAY. You must reenter program.

Life Insurance: Its Rate of Return

Five (5) Year Measurement

ON — XEQ — ALPHA — SIZE — ALPHA — 023
XEQ — ALPHA — IRR — ALPHA
CLR ?   R/S
GROUPS ?   N   R/S
TOTL CFS = ?   6   R/S

CF 1	CF AMT = ?	175	CHS	R/S
CF 2	CF AMT = ?	198	CHS	R/S
CF 3	CF AMT = ?	224	CHS	R/S
CF 4	CF AMT = ?	253	CHS	R/S
CF 5	CF AMT = ?	285	CHS	R/S
CF 6	CF AMT = ?	100,000		R/S

CF CHANGES ?   N   R/S

Now calculating — will take a few minutes.

IRR = 227.34%   IRR = Rate of Return

CF 6 is the 5th-year death benefit.

CLEAR DISPLAY. You must reenter the program.

Calculate the Rate of Return for Life Insurance

Fifteen (15) Year Management

ON — XEQ — ALPHA — SIZE — ALPHA — 033
XEQ — ALPHA — IRR — ALPHA
CLR ?   R/S
GROUPS ?   N   R/S
TOTL CFS = ?   16   R/S

CF 1	CF AMT = ?	175	CHS	R/S
CF 2	CF AMT = ?	198	CHS	R/S
CF 3	CF AMT = ?	224	CHS	R/S
CF 4	CF AMT = ?	253	CHS	R/S
CF 5	CF AMT = ?	285	CHS	R/S
CF 6	CF AMT = ?	307	CHS	R/S
CF 7	CF AMT = ?	328	CHS	R/S
CF 8	CF AMT = ?	351	CHS	R/S
CF 9	CF AMT = ?	376	CHS	R/S
CF 10	CF AMT = ?	404	CHS	R/S
CF 11	CF AMT = ?	434	CHS	R/S
CF 12	CF AMT = ?	467	CHS	R/S
CF 13	CF AMT = ?	505	CHS	R/S
CF 14	CF AMT = ?	545	CHS	R/S
CF 15	CF AMT = ?	590	CHS	R/S
CF 16	CF AMT = ?	100,000		R/S

CF CHANGES ?   N   R/S

Now calculating — will take a few minutes.

IRR = 37.06%   IRR = Rate of Return

CF 16 is the 15th-year death benefit.

CLEAR DISPLAY. You must reenter the program.

Life Insurance: Its Rate of Return

Thirty (30) Year Measurement

ON — XEQ — ALPHA — SIZE — ALPHA — 048
XEQ — ALPHA — IRR — ALPHA
CLR ?   R/S
GROUP ?   N   R/S
TOTL CFS = ?   31   R/S

CF 1	CF AMT = ?	175	CHS	R/S
CF 2	CF AMT = ?	198	CHS	R/S
CF 3	CF AMT = ?	224	CHS	R/S
CF 4	CF AMT = ?	253	CHS	R/S
CF 5	CF AMT = ?	285	CHS	R/S
CF 6	CF AMT = ?	307	CHS	R/S
CF 7	CF AMT = ?	328	CHS	R/S
CF 8	CF AMT = ?	351	CHS	R/S
CF 9	CF AMT = ?	376	CHS	R/S
CF 10	CF AMT = ?	404	CHS	R/S
CF 11	CF AMT = ?	434	CHS	R/S
CF 12	CF AMT = ?	467	CHS	R/S
CF 13	CF AMT = ?	505	CHS	R/S
CF 14	CF AMT = ?	545	CHS	R/S
CF 15	CF AMT = ?	590	CHS	R/S
CF 16	CF AMT = ?	640	CHS	R/S
CF 17	CF AMT = ?	699	CHS	R/S
CF 18	CF AMT = ?	755	CHS	R/S
CF 19	CF AMT = ?	816	CHS	R/S
CF 20	CF AMT = ?	884	CHS	R/S
CF 21	CF AMT = ?	958	CHS	R/S
CF 22	CF AMT = ?	1,038	CHS	R/S
CF 23	CF AMT = ?	1,123	CHS	R/S
CF 24	CF AMT = ?	1,214	CHS	R/S
CF 25	CF AMT = ?	1,317	CHS	R/S
CF 26	CF AMT = ?	1,434	CHS	R/S
CF 27	CF AMT = ?	1,570	CHS	R/S
CF 28	CF AMT = ?	1,678	CHS	R/S
CF 29	CF AMT = ?	1,835	CHS	R/S
CF 30	CF AMT = ?	2,009	CHS	R/S
CF 31	CF AMT = ?	100,000		R/S

CF CHANGES ?   N   R/S

Now calculating — will take a few minutes.

IRR = 11.27%   IRR = Rate of Return

CF 31 is the 30th-year death benefit.

CLEAR DISPLAY. You must reenter the program.

Calculate the Rate of Return for Life Insurance

Forty-five (45) Year Measurement

ON — XEQ — ALPHA — SIZE — ALPHA — 063
XEQ — ALPHA — IRR — ALPHA
CLR ?   R/S
GROUPS ?   N   R/S
TOTL CFS = ?   46   R/S

CF 1	CF AMT = ?	175	CHS	R/S
CF 2	CF AMT = ?	198	CHS	R/S
CF 3	CF AMT = ?	224	CHS	R/S
CF 4	CF AMT = ?	253	CHS	R/S
CF 5	CF AMT = ?	285	CHS	R/S
CF 6	CF AMT = ?	307	CHS	R/S
CF 7	CF AMT = ?	328	CHS	R/S
CF 8	CF AMT = ?	351	CHS	R/S
CF 9	CF AMT = ?	376	CHS	R/S
CF 10	CF AMT = ?	404	CHS	R/S
CF 11	CF AMT = ?	434	CHS	R/S
CF 12	CF AMT = ?	467	CHS	R/S
CF 13	CF AMT = ?	505	CHS	R/S
CF 14	CF AMT = ?	545	CHS	R/S
CF 15	CF AMT = ?	590	CHS	R/S
CF 16	CF AMT = ?	640	CHS	R/S
CF 17	CF AMT = ?	699	CHS	R/S
CF 18	CF AMT = ?	755	CHS	R/S
CF 19	CF AMT = ?	816	CHS	R/S
CF 20	CF AMT = ?	884	CHS	R/S
CF 21	CF AMT = ?	958	CHS	R/S
CF 22	CF AMT = ?	1,038	CHS	R/S
CF 23	CF AMT = ?	1,123	CHS	R/S
CF 24	CF AMT = ?	1,214	CHS	R/S
CF 25	CF AMT = ?	1,317	CHS	R/S
CF 26	CF AMT = ?	1,434	CHS	R/S
CF 27	CF AMT = ?	1,570	CHS	R/S
CF 28	CF AMT = ?	1,678	CHS	R/S
CF 29	CF AMT = ?	1,835	CHS	R/S
CF 30	CF AMT = ?	2,009	CHS	R/S
CF 31	CF AMT = ?	2,194	CHS	R/S
CF 32	CF AMT = ?	2,389	CHS	R/S
CF 33	CF AMT = ?	2,588	CHS	R/S
CF 34	CF AMT = ?	2,792	CHS	R/S
CF 35	CF AMT = ?	3,007	CHS	R/S
CF 36	CF AMT = ?	3,240	CHS	R/S
CF 37	CF AMT = ?	3,629	CHS	R/S
CF 38	CF AMT = ?	4,012	CHS	R/S
CF 39	CF AMT = ?	4,414	CHS	R/S

Life Insurance: Its Rate of Return

CF 40	CF AMT = ?	4,829	CHS	R/S
CF 41	CF AMT = ?	5,260	CHS	R/S
CF 42	CF AMT = ?	5,610	CHS	R/S
CF 43	CF AMT = ?	6,056	CHS	R/S
CF 44	CF AMT = ?	6,561	CHS	R/S
CF 45	CF AMT = ?	7,114	CHS	R/S
CF 46	CF AMT = ?	100,000		R/S

CF CHANGES ?   N   R/S

Now calculating — will take a few minutes.

IRR = 1.16%   IRR = Rate of Return

CF 46 is the 45th-year death benefit.

CLEAR DISPLAY.

HOW TO CALCULATE THE INSURED'S RATE OF RETURN FOR YEARLY RENEWABLE TERM WITHOUT REISSUE PROVISION

It is not necessary to calculate the insured's rate of return for Yearly Renewable Term without Reissue Provision. There is no future value to the insured. Therefore, the insured's rate of return is always −100% compound.

Calculate the Rate of Return for Life Insurance

LEVEL TERM LEDGER STATEMENT

Plan: YEARLY RENEWABLE TERM TO 100+
Issue Age: 35 Male
Class: PREFERRED STANDARD

Face Amount: $100,000

Policy Year	Annual Premium*	Dividend End of Prior Year**	Net Annual Premium**	Policy Year	Annual Premium*	Dividend End of Prior Year**	Net Annual Premium**
1	175	0	175	24	1431	217	1214
2	198	0	198	25	1559	242	1317
3	224	0	224	26	1704	270	1434
4	253	0	253	27	1872	302	1570
5	285	0	285	28	2068	390	1678
6	340	33	307	29	2294	459	1835
7	364	36	328	30	2548	539	2009
8	390	39	351	31	2823	629	2194
9	419	43	376	32	3115	726	2389
10	451	47	404	33	3418	830	2588
11	485	51	434	34	3729	937	2792
12	523	56	467	35	4054	1047	3007
13	566	61	505	36	4402	1162	3420
14	612	67	545	37	4914	1285	3629
15	664	74	590	38	5479	1467	4012
16	721	81	640	39	6081	1667	4414
17	785	86	699	40	6709	1880	4829
18	855	100	755	41	7362	2102	5260
19	932	116	816	42	7943	2333	5610
20	1017	133	884	43	8595	2539	6056
21	1109	151	958	44	9331	2770	6561
22	1209	171	1038	45	10144	3030	7114
23	1316	193	1123				

Life Insurance: Its Rate of Return

Summary	Total Annual Premiums+	Total Annual Dividends**	Total Net Premiums**
5 years	1135	33	1102
10 Years	3099	249	2850
15 Years	5949	588	5361
20 Years	10259	1174	9085
Age 60	16883	2267	14616
Age 65	27369	4586	22783
Age 70	44508	9288	35220

New England Mutual Life Insurance Company

Calculate the Rate of Return for Life Insurance

HOW TO CALCULATE THE BENEFICIARY'S RATE OF RETURN FOR WHOLE LIFE (ORDINARY LIFE)

Here is a series of unequal present value payments (premiums) which change each and every year. Future value (the death benefit) remains the same for each year at $100,000. The time span is the number of years you wish to measure.

Note: Some years have a "no cost" payment. This is because the declared dividend exceeds the annual premium. *Do not use "CHS" after the dollar amount in those years.*

Program: MONEY

One (1) Year Measurement

ON — XEQ — ALPHA — SIZE — ALPHA — 015
XEQ — ALPHA — MONEY — ALPHA
CLR ?   R/S
END ?   R/S
BEGIN   READY

```
           1,301      CHS  PMT
               1      N
         100,000      FV
               I      Now calculating.
               I  =   7,586.40%
               I  =   Rate of Return
```

CLEAR DISPLAY. You now change programs.

Life Insurance: Its Rate of Return

Program: IRR

Five (5) Year Measurement

ON — XEQ — ALPHA — SIZE — ALPHA — 023
XEQ — ALPHA — IRR — ALPHA
CLR ?   R/S
GROUPS ?   N   R/S
TOTL CFS = ?   6   R/S

CF 1	CF AMT = ?	1,301	CHS	R/S
CF 2	CF AMT = ?	1,242	CHS	R/S
CF 3	CF AMT = ?	1,183	CHS	R/S
CF 4	CF AMT = ?	1,120	CHS	R/S
CF 5	CF AMT = ?	1,055	CHS	R/S
CF 6	CF AMT = ?	100,000		R/S

CF CHANGES ?   N   R/S

Now calculating — will take a few minutes.

IRR = 112.33%   IRR = Rate of Return

CF 6 is the 5th-year death benefit.

CLEAR DISPLAY. You must reenter program.

Calculate the Rate of Return for Life Insurance

Fifteen (15) Year Measurement

ON — XEQ — ALPHA — SIZE — ALPHA — 033
XEQ — ALPHA — IRR — ALPHA
CLR ?   R/S
GROUPS ?   N   R/S
TOTL CFS = ?   16   R/S

CF 1	CF AMT = ?	1,301	CHS	R/S
CF 2	CF AMT = ?	1,242	CHS	R/S
CF 3	CF AMT = ?	1,183	CHS	R/S
CF 4	CF AMT = ?	1,120	CHS	R/S
CF 5	CF AMT = ?	1,055	CHS	R/S
CF 6	CF AMT = ?	987	CHS	R/S
CF 7	CF AMT = ?	916	CHS	R/S
CF 8	CF AMT = ?	843	CHS	R/S
CF 9	CF AMT = ?	767	CHS	R/S
CF 10	CF AMT = ?	689	CHS	R/S
CF 11	CF AMT = ?	608	CHS	R/S
CF 12	CF AMT = ?	524	CHS	R/S
CF 13	CF AMT = ?	438	CHS	R/S
CF 14	CF AMT = ?	335	CHS	R/S
CF 15	CF AMT = ?	229	CHS	R/S
CF 16	CF AMT = ?	100,000		R/S

CF CHANGES ?   N   R/S

Now calculating — will take a few minutes.

IRR = 21.08%   IRR = Rate of Retrn

CF 16 is the 15th-year death benefit.

CLEAR DISPLAY. You must reenter program.

Life Insurance: Its Rate of Return

Thirty (30) Year Measurement

ON — XEQ — ALPHA — SIZE — ALPHA - 048
XEQ — ALPHA — IRR — ALPHA
CLR ?   R/S
GROUPS ?   N   R/S
TOTL CFS = ?   31   R/S

CF 1	CF AMT = ?	1,301	CHS	R/S
CF 2	CF AMT = ?	1,242	CHS	R/S
CF 3	CF AMT = ?	1,183	CHS	R/S
CF 4	CF AMT = ?	1,120	CHS	R/S
CF 5	CF AMT = ?	1,055	CHS	R/S
CF 6	CF AMT = ?	987	CHS	R/S
CF 7	CF AMT = ?	916	CHS	R/S
CF 8	CF AMT = ?	843	CHS	R/S
CF 9	CF AMT = ?	767	CHS	R/S
CF 10	CF AMT = ?	689	CHS	R/S
CF 11	CF AMT = ?	608	CHS	R/S
CF 12	CF AMT = ?	524	CHS	R/S
CF 13	CF AMT = ?	438	CHS	R/S
CF 14	CF AMT = ?	335	CHS	R/S
CF 15	CF AMT = ?	229	CHS	R/S
CF 16	CF AMT = ?	129	CHS	R/S
CF 17	CF AMT = ?	35	CHS	R/S
CF 18	CF AMT = ?	61		R/S
CF 19	CF AMT = ?	153		R/S
CF 20	CF AMT = ?	246		R/S
CF 21	CF AMT = ?	338		R/S
CF 22	CF AMT = ?	455		R/S
CF 23	CF AMT = ?	565		R/S
CF 24	CF AMT = ?	677		R/S
CF 25	CF AMT = ?	792		R/S
CF 26	CF AMT = ?	908		R/S
CF 27	CF AMT = ?	1,027		R/S
CF 28	CF AMT = ?	1,146		R/S
CF 29	CF AMT = ?	1,263		R/S
CF 30	CF AMT = ?	1,381		R/S
CF 31	CF AMT = ?	100,000		R/S

CF CHANGES ?   N   R/S

Now calculating — will take a few minutes.

IRR = 9.19%   IRR = Rate of Return

CF 31 is the 30th-year death benefit.

CLEAR DISPLAY. You must reenter program.

Calculate the Rate of Return for Life Insurance

Forty-five (45) Year Measurement

ON — XEQ — ALPHA — SIZE — ALPHA — 063
XEQ — ALPHA — IRR — ALPHA
CLR ?   R/S
GROUPS ?   N   R/S
TOTL CFS = ?   46   R/S

CF 1	CF AMT = ?	1,301	CHS	R/S
CF 2	CF AMT = ?	1,242	CHS	R/S
CF 3	CF AMT = ?	1,183	CHS	R/S
CF 4	CF AMT = ?	1,120	CHS	R/S
CF 5	CF AMT = ?	1,055	CHS	R/S
CF 6	CF AMT = ?	987	CHS	R/S
CF 7	CF AMT = ?	916	CHS	R/S
CF 8	CF AMT = ?	843	CHS	R/S
CF 9	CF AMT = ?	767	CHS	R/S
CF 10	CF AMT = ?	689	CHS	R/S
CF 11	CF AMT = ?	608	CHS	R/S
CF 12	CF AMT = ?	524	CHS	R/S
CF 13	CF AMT = ?	438	CHS	R/S
CF 14	CF AMT = ?	335	CHS	R/S
CF 15	CF AMT = ?	229	CHS	R/S
CF 16	CF AMT = ?	129	CHS	R/S
CF 17	CF AMT = ?	35	CHS	R/S
CF 18	CF AMT = ?	61		R/S
CF 19	CF AMT = ?	153		R/S
CF 20	CF AMT = ?	246		R/S
CF 21	CF AMT = ?	338		R/S
CF 22	CF AMT = ?	455		R/S
CF 23	CF AMT = ?	565		R/S
CF 24	CF AMT = ?	677		R/S
CF 25	CF AMT = ?	792		R/S
CF 26	CF AMT = ?	908		R/S
CF 27	CF AMT = ?	1,027		R/S
CF 28	CF AMT = ?	1,146		R/S
CF 29	CF AMT = ?	1,263		R/S
CF 30	CF AMT = ?	1,381		R/S
CF 31	CF AMT = ?	1,500		R/S
CF 32	CF AMT = ?	1,622		R/S
CF 33	CF AMT = ?	1,756		R/S
CF 34	CF AMT = ?	1,894		R/S
CF 35	CF AMT = ?	2,035		R/S
CF 36	CF AMT = ?	2,176		R/S
CF 37	CF AMT = ?	2,316		R/S
CF 38	CF AMT = ?	2,455		R/S
CF 39	CF AMT = ?	2,583		R/S

Life Insurance: Its Rate of Return

CF 40	CF AMT = ?	2,705	R/S
CF 41	CF AMT = ?	2,821	R/S
CF 42	CF AMT = ?	2,939	R/S
CF 43	CF AMT = ?	3,055	R/S
CF 44	CF AMT = ?	3,172	R/S
CF 45	CF AMT = ?	3,293	R/S
CF 46	CF AMT = ?	100,000	R/S

CF CHANGES ?   N   R/S

Now calculating — will take a few minutes.

IRR = 7.14%   IRR = Rate of Return

CF 46 is the 45th-year death benefit.

CLEAR DISPLAY.

HOW TO CALCULATE THE INSURED'S RATE OF RETURN FOR WHOLE LIFE (ORDINARY LIFE)

Here is a series of unequal present value payments (premiums) which change each and every year. Future value (cash value) changes each and every year. The time span is the number of years you wish to measure.

Program: IRR

One (1) Year Measurement

It is not necessary to do this calculation as the future value to the insured is zero (0) and the rate of return is –100% compound.

Five (5) Year Measurement

ON — XEQ — ALPHA — SIZE — ALPHA — 023
XEQ — ALPHA — IRR — ALPHA
CLR ?   R/S
GROUPS ?   N   R/S
TOTL CFS = ?   6   R/S

CF 1	CF AMT = ?	1,301	CHS	R/S
CF 2	CF AMT = ?	1,242	CHS	R/S
CF 3	CF AMT = ?	1,183	CHS	R/S
CF 4	CF AMT = ?	1,120	CHS	R/S
CF 5	CF AMT = ?	1,055	CHS	R/S
CF 6	CF AMT = ?	4,997		R/S

CF CHANGES ?   N   R/S

Now calculating — will take a few minutes.

IRR = –5.31%   IRR = Rate of Return

CF 6 is the 5th-year cash value.

CLEAR DISPLAY. You must reenter program.

Life Insurance: Its Rate of Return

Fifteen (15) Year Measurement

ON — XEQ — ALPHA — SIZE — ALPHA — 033
XEQ — ALPHA — IRR — ALPHA
CLR ?   R/S
GROUPS ?   N   R/S
TOTL CFS = ?   16   R/S

CF 1	CF AMT = ?	1,301	CHS	R/S
CF 2	CF AMT = ?	1,242	CHS	R/S
CF 3	CF AMT = ?	1,183	CHS	R/S
CF 4	CF AMT = ?	1,120	CHS	R/S
CF 5	CF AMT = ?	1,055	CHS	R/S
CF 6	CF AMT = ?	987	CHS	R/S
CF 7	CF AMT = ?	916	CHS	R/S
CF 8	CF AMT = ?	843	CHS	R/S
CF 9	CF AMT = ?	767	CHS	R/S
CF 10	CF AMT = ?	689	CHS	R/S
CF 11	CF AMT = ?	608	CHS	R/S
CF 12	CF AMT = ?	524	CHS	R/S
CF 13	CF AMT = ?	438	CHS	R/S
CF 14	CF AMT = ?	335	CHS	R/S
CF 15	CF AMT = ?	229	CHS	R/S
CF 16	CF AMT = ?	19,912		R/S

CF CHANGES ?   N   R/S

Now calculating — will take a few minutes.

IRR = 4.95%   IRR = Rate of Return

CF 16 is the 15th-year cash value.

CLEAR DISPLAY. You must reenter program.

Calculate the Rate of Return for Life Insurance

Thirty (30) Year Measurement

ON — XEQ — ALPHA — SIZE — ALPHA - 048
XEQ — ALPHA — IRR — ALPHA
CLR ? R/S
GROUPS ? N R/S
TOTL CFS = ? 31 R/S

CF 1	CF AMT = ?	1,301	CHS	R/S
CF 2	CF AMT = ?	1,242	CHS	R/S
CF 3	CF AMT = ?	1,183	CHS	R/S
CF 4	CF AMT = ?	1,120	CHS	R/S
CF 5	CF AMT = ?	1,055	CHS	R/S
CF 6	CF AMT = ?	987	CHS	R/S
CF 7	CF AMT = ?	916	CHS	R/S
CF 8	CF AMT = ?	843	CHS	R/S
CF 9	CF AMT = ?	767	CHS	R/S
CF 10	CF AMT = ?	689	CHS	R/S
CF 11	CF AMT = ?	608	CHS	R/S
CF 12	CF AMT = ?	524	CHS	R/S
CF 13	CF AMT = ?	438	CHS	R/S
CF 14	CF AMT = ?	335	CHS	R/S
CF 15	CF AMT = ?	229	CHS	R/S
CF 16	CF AMT = ?	129	CHS	R/S
CF 17	CF AMT = ?	35	CHS	R/S
CF 18	CF AMT = ?	61		R/S
CF 19	CF AMT = ?	153		R/S
CF 20	CF AMT = ?	246		R/S
CF 21	CF AMT = ?	338		R/S
CF 22	CF AMT = ?	455		R/S
CF 23	CF AMT = ?	565		R/S
CF 24	CF AMT = ?	677		R/S
CF 25	CF AMT = ?	792		R/S
CF 26	CF AMT = ?	908		R/S
CF 27	CF AMT = ?	1,027		R/S
CF 28	CF AMT = ?	1,146		R/S
CF 29	CF AMT = ?	1,263		R/S
CF 30	CF AMT = ?	1,381		R/S
CF 31	CF AMT = ?	46,863		R/S

CF CHANGES ? N R/S

Now calculating — will take a few minutes.

IRR = 6.43%   IRR = Rate of Return

CF 31 is the 30th-year cash value.

CLEAR DISPLAY. You must reenter program.

Life Insurance: Its Rate of Return

Forty-five (45) Year Measurement

ON — XEQ — ALPHA — SIZE — ALPHA — 063
XEQ — ALPHA — IRR — ALPHA
CLR ?   R/S
GROUPS ?   N   R/S
TOTL CFS = ?   46   R/S

CF 1	CF AMT = ?	1,301	CHS	R/S
CF 2	CF AMT = ?	1,242	CHS	R/S
CF 3	CF AMT = ?	1,183	CHS	R/S
CF 4	CF AMT = ?	1,120	CHS	R/S
CF 5	CF AMT = ?	1,055	CHS	R/S
CF 6	CF AMT = ?	987	CHS	R/S
CF 7	CF AMT = ?	916	CHS	R/S
CF 8	CF AMT = ?	843	CHS	R/S
CF 9	CF AMT = ?	767	CHS	R/S
CF 10	CF AMT = ?	689	CHS	R/S
CF 11	CF AMT = ?	608	CHS	R/S
CF 12	CF AMT = ?	524	CHS	R/S
CF 13	CF AMT = ?	438	CHS	R/S
CF 14	CF AMT = ?	335	CHS	R/S
CF 15	CF AMT = ?	229	CHS	R/S
CF 16	CF AMT = ?	129	CHS	R/S
CF 17	CF AMT = ?	35	CHS	R/S
CF 18	CF AMT = ?	61		R/S
CF 19	CF AMT = ?	153		R/S
CF 20	CF AMT = ?	246		R/S
CF 21	CF AMT = ?	338		R/S
CF 22	CF AMT = ?	455		R/S
CF 23	CF AMT = ?	565		R/S
CF 24	CF AMT = ?	677		R/S
CF 25	CF AMT = ?	792		R/S
CF 26	CF AMT = ?	908		R/S
CF 27	CF AMT = ?	1,027		R/S
CF 28	CF AMT = ?	1,146		R/S
CF 29	CF AMT = ?	1,263		R/S
CF 30	CF AMT = ?	1,381		R/S
CF 31	CF AMT = ?	1,500		R/S
CF 32	CF AMT = ?	1,622		R/S
CF 33	CF AMT = ?	1,756		R/S
CF 34	CF AMT = ?	1,894		R/S
CF 35	CF AMT = ?	2,035		R/S
CF 36	CF AMT = ?	2,176		R/S
CF 37	CF AMT = ?	2,316		R/S
CF 38	CF AMT = ?	2,455		R/S
CF 39	CF AMT = ?	2,583		R/S

Calculate the Rate of Return for Life Insurance

CF 40	CF AMT = ?	2,705	R/S
CF 41	CF AMT = ?	2,821	R/S
CF 42	CF AMT = ?	2,939	R/S
CF 43	CF AMT = ?	3,055	R/S
CF 44	CF AMT = ?	3,172	R/S
CF 45	CF AMT = ?	3,293	R/S
CF 46	CF AMT = ?	71,736	R/S

CF CHANGES ? N R/S

Now calculating — will take a few minutes.

IRR = 6.65%   IRR = Rate of Return

CF 46 is the 45th-year cash value.

CLEAR DISPLAY.

Life Insurance: Its Rate of Return

STANDARD LEDGER STATEMENT

Plan: ORDINARY LIFE+
Issue Age: 35 MALE
Class: PREFERRED STANDARD

Annual Premium: $1,301.00
Face Amount: $100,000

Policy Year	Annual Dividend*	Net Annual Premium*	Annual Increase In Guaranteed Cash Value	Net Premium* Less Cash Value Increase	Guaranteed Cash Value
1	0	1301	0	1301	0
2	59	1242	1215	27	1215
3	118	1183	1223	40–	2438
4	181	1120	1261	141–	3699
5	246	1055	1298	243–	4997
6	314	987	1333	346–	6330
7	385	916	1369	453–	7699
8	458	843	1405	562–	9104
9	534	767	1441	674–	10545
10	612	689	1477	788–	12022
11	693	608	1512	904–	13534
12	777	524	1547	1023–	15081
13	863	438	1579	1141–	16660
14	966	335	1611	1276–	18271
15	1072	229	1641	1412–	19912
16	1172	129	1669	1540–	21581
17	1266	35	1695	1660–	23276
18	1362	61–	1721	1782–	24997
19	1454	153–	1745	1898–	26742
20	1547	246–	1767	2013–	28509

Calculate the Rate of Return for Life Insurance

Policy Year	Annual Dividend*	Net Annual Premium*	Annual Increase In Guaranteed Cash Value	Net Premium* Less Cash Value Increase	Guaranteed Cash Value
21	1639	338–	1788	2126–	30297
22	1756	455–	1806	2261–	32103
23	1866	565–	1822	2387–	33925
24	1978	677–	1834	2511–	35759
25	2093	792–	1844	2636–	37603
26	2209	908–	1851	2759–	39454
27	2328	1027–	1854	2881–	41308
28	2447	1146–	1855	3001–	43163
29	2564	1263–	1853	3116–	45016
30	2682	1381–	1847	3228–	46863
31	2801	1500–	1836	3336–	48699
32	2923	1622–	1819	3441–	50518
33	3057	1756–	1797	3553–	52315
34	3195	1894–	1767	3661–	54082
35	3336	2035–	1734	3769–	55816
36	3477	2176–	1699	3875–	57515
37	3617	2316–	1667	3983–	59182
38	3756	2455–	1643	4098–	60825
39	3884	2583–	1624	4207–	62449
40	4006	2705–	1611	4316–	64060
41	4122	2821–	1596	4417–	65656
42	4240	2939–	1576	4515–	67232
43	4356	3055–	1546	4601–	68778
44	4473	3172–	1505	4677–	70283
45	4594	3293–	1453	4746–	71736

Dividends* used to reduce premiums. Any excess dividend is assumed payable in cash and is shown as a negative net annual premium.

* Illustrated dividends assume no loans on the policy. Policy loans will reduce dividends.

Life Insurance: Its Rate of Return

Summary #	Guaranteed Cash Value	Total Net Premiums*	Total Net Premiums* Less Cash Value	Guaranteed Paid-up Insurance
5 Years	4997	5587	590	17754
10 Years	12022	9410	2612–	35929
15 Years	19912	11065	8847–	50503
20 Years	28509	10302	18207–	62072
Age 65	46863	588	46275–	78352

Terminal Dividend* 15th yr: $ 249.00   20th yr: $ 2067.00

Interest-Adjusted Indexes* based on a 5.00% interest rate, for basic policy only:

Life Insurance Net Payment Cost Index	10 yrs: $ 9.85	20 yrs: $ 6.80	Age 65: $ 3.96
Life Insurance Surrender Cost Index	10 yrs: $ 0.75	20 yrs: $ 2.00–	Age 65: $ 3.24–
Equivalent Level Annual Dividend	10 yrs: $ 3.16	20 yrs: $ 6.21	Age 65: $ 9.05

Premium Information:
	Annual	Semi-annual	Quarterly	Monthly
ORDINARY LIFE	$1,301.00	$666.95	$338.56	$114.45

* Includes dividend values. Dividends are a return of part of the premium and primarily depend on investment earnings, mortality and expense experience. Dividends are computed on current dividend scale and are neither guarantees nor estimates for the future. A Terminal Dividend is payable upon surrender, lapse or death, after at least 15 policy years, but only if declared by the Company at such time, and is included in the Interest-Adjusted Surrender Cost Index.

+ The values shown in the ledger assume an annual mode of premium payment and a(n) 8.00% fixed policy loan interest rate applied in arrears. The issuance of any policies or riders is subject to the Company's regular underwriting practices. The amounts of coverage and premiums for any policies or riders, if issued, may differ from those illustrated.

\# Summary Values are calculated as of the end of the year.

New England Mutual Life Insurance Company

Calculate the Rate of Return for Life Insurance

HOW TO CALCULATE THE BENEFICIARY'S RATE OF RETURN FOR ADJUSTABLE PREMIUM WHOLE LIFE (UNIVERSAL LIFE), OPTION A

Present value payment (premium) is $1,008 each and every year. Future value (the death benefit) never exceeds $100,000. The time span is the number of years you wish to measure.

Program: MONEY

One (1) Year Measurement

ON — XEQ — ALPHA — SIZE — ALPHA - 015
XEQ — ALPHA — MONEY — ALPHA
CLR ?   R/S
END ?   N   R/S
BEGIN   READY

1,008	CHS	PMT
1	N	
100,000	FV	
I	Now calculating.	
I =	9,820.63%	
I =	Rate of Return	

CLEAR DISPLAY. You must reenter program.

Life Insurance: Its Rate of Return

Five (5) Year Measurement

ON — XEQ — ALPHA — SIZE — ALPHA - 015
XEQ — ALPHA — MONEY — ALPHA
CLR ? R/S
END ? N R/S
BEGIN   READY

        1,008   CHS PMT
           5   N
    100,000   FV
           I   Now calculating.
           I = 123.55%
           I = Rate of Return

CLEAR DISPLAY. You must reenter program.

Fifteen (15) Year Measurement

ON — XEQ — ALPHA — SIZE — ALPHA — 015
XEQ — ALPHA — MONEY — ALPHA
CLR ? R/S
END ? N R/S
BEGIN   READY

        1,008   CHS PMT
          15   N
    100,000   FV
           I   Now calculating.
           I = 21.50%
           I = Rate of Return

CLEAR DISPLAY. You must reenter program.

Calculate the Rate of Return for Life Insurance

Thirty (30) Year Measurement

ON — XEQ — ALPHA — SIZE — ALPHA — 015
XEQ — ALPHA — MONEY — ALPHA
CLR ?   R/S
END ?   N   R/S
BEGIN   READY

1,008	CHS	PMT
30	N	
100,000	FV	
I	Now calculating.	
I =	6.90%	
I =	Rate of Return	

CLEAR DISPLAY. You must reenter program.

Forty-five (45) Year Measurement

ON — XEQ — ALPHA — SIZE — ALPHA — 015
XEQ — ALPHA — MONEY — ALPHA
CLR ?   R/S
END ?   N   R/S
BEGIN   READY

1,008	CHS	PMT
45	N	
100,000	FV	
I	Now calculating.	
I =	3.14%	
I =	Rate of Return	

CLEAR DISPLAY.

Life Insurance: Its Rate of Return

HOW TO CALCULATE THE INSURED'S RATE OF RETURN FOR ADJUSTABLE PREMIUM WHOLE LIFE (UNIVERSAL LIFE), OPTION A

Note: You calculate the insured's rate of return in the exact manner as the beneficiary's rate of return. However, there is a different future value amount for the insured.

One (1) Year Measurement

ON — XEQ — ALPHA — SIZE — ALPHA — 015
XEQ — ALPHA — MONEY — ALPHA
CLR ?   R/S
END ?   N   R/S
BEGIN   READY

               1,008   CHS   PMT
                   1   N
                 35   FV
                 I   Now calculating.
                 I = 96.53%
                 I = Rate of Return

CLEAR DISPLAY. You must reenter program.

Calculate the Rate of Return for Life Insurance

Five (5) Year Measurement

ON — XEQ — ALPHA — SIZE — ALPHA — 015
XEQ — ALPHA — MONEY — ALPHA
CLR ?   R/S
END ?   N   R/S
BEGIN   READY

        1,008   CHS   PMT
           5   N
        3,815   FV
           I   Now calculating.
           I   =   –9.14%
           I   =   Rate of Return

CLEAR DISPLAY. You must reenter program.

Fifteen (15) Year Measurement

ON — XEQ — ALPHA — SIZE — ALPHA — 015
XEQ — ALPHA — MONEY — ALPHA
CLR ?   R/S
END ?   N   R/S
BEGIN   READY

        1,008   CHS   PMT
          15   N
     21,815   FV
           I   Now calculating.
           I   =   4.46%
           I   =   Rate of Return

CLEAR DISPLAY. You must reenter program.

Life Insurance: Its Rate of Return

Thirty (30) Year Measurement

ON — XEQ — ALPHA — SIZE — ALPHA — 015
XEQ — ALPHA — MONEY — ALPHA
CLR ?   R/S
END ?   N   R/S
BEGIN   READY

1,008	CHS PMT
30	N
112,275	FV
I	Now calculating.
I =	7.51%
I =	Rate of Return

CLEAR DISPLAY. You must reenter program.

Forty-five (45) Year Measurement

ON — XEQ — ALPHA — SIZE — ALPHA — 015
XEQ — ALPHA — MONEY — ALPHA
CLR ?   R/S
END ?   N   R/S
BEGIN   READY

1,008	CHS PMT
45	N
484,590	FV
I	Now calculating.
I =	8.45%
I =	Rate of Return

CLEAR DISPLAY.

Calculate the Rate of Return for Life Insurance

Plan: FLEXIBLE PREMIUM ADJUSTABLE LIFE
Issue Age: 35 MALE
Class: PREFERRED

Initial Face Amount: $100,000

Year	Age	Annual Premium	10.00% Basis (current) Cash Value	10.00% Basis (current) Death Benefit	4.50% Basis (guaranteed) Cash Value	4.50% Basis (guaranteed) Death Benefit
1	35	1,008.00	35	100,000	30	100,000
2	36	1,008.00	860	100,000	734	100,000
3	37	1,008.00	1,760	100,000	1,458	100,000
4	38	1,008.00	2,742	100,000	2,194	100,000
5	39	1,008.00	3,815	100,000	2,941	100,000
6	40	1,008.00	4,986	100,000	3,701	100,000
7	41	1,008.00	6,265	100,000	4,463	100,000
8	42	1,008.00	7,663	100,000	5,227	100,000
9	43	1,008.00	9,190	100,000	5,995	100,000
10	44	1,008.00	10,857	100,000	6,766	100,000
11	45	1,008.00	12,679	100,000	7,531	100,000
12	46	1,008.00	14,667	100,000	8,289	100,000
13	47	1,008.00	16,839	100,000	9,042	100,000
14	48	1,008.00	19,216	100,000	9,778	100,000
15	49	1,008.00	21,815	100,000	10,498	100,000
16	50	1,008.00	24,658	100,000	11,179	100,000
17	51	1,008.00	27,772	100,000	11,833	100,000
18	52	1,008.00	31,187	100,000	12,447	100,000
19	53	1,008.00	34,933	100,000	13,009	100,000
20	54	1,008.00	39,048	100,000	13,519	100,000
21	55	1,008.00	43,576	100,000	13,963	100,000

Life Insurance: Its Rate of Return

Year	Age	Annual Premium	10.00% Basis (current) Cash Value	10.00% Basis (current) Death Benefit	4.50% Basis (guaranteed) Cash Value	4.50% Basis (guaranteed) Death Benefit
22	56	1,008.00	48,559	100,000	14,328	100,000
23	57	1,008.00	54,050	100,000	14,588	100,000
24	58	1,008.00	60,108	100,000	14,740	100,000
25	59	1,008.00	66,798	100,000	14,765	100,000
26	60	1,008.00	74,196	100,000	14,635	100,000
27	61	1,008.00	82,389	100,000	14,328	100,000
28	62	1,008.00	91,443	107,902	13,820	100,000
29	63	1,008.00	101,377	118,611	13,086	100,000
30	64	1,008.00	112,275	130,239	12,071	100,000
31	65	1,008.00	124,229	142,864	10,728	100,000
32	66	1,008.00	137,342	156,570	9,002	100,000
33	67	1,008.00	151,727	171,451	6,827	100,000
34	68	1,008.00	167,508	187,609	4,116	100,000
35	69	1,008.00	184,825	205,156	763	100,000
36	70	1,008.00	203,831	224,214	**LAPSE	**LAPSE
37	71	1,008.00	224,697	244,920	0	0
38	72	1,008.00	247,614	267,423	0	0
39	73	1,008.00	272,794	291,890	0	0
40	74	1,008.00	300,475	318,504	0	0
45	79	1,008.00	484,590	508,820	0	0
50	84	0.00	763,856	802,049	0	0
55	89	0.00	1,183,444	1,242,617	0	0
60	94	0.00	1,804,161	1,894,370	0	0

Calculate the Rate of Return for Life Insurance

**The policy will terminate at this time unless the plan premium is increased.

Current interest is credited on cash value over $500. Guaranteed interest is credited on the first $500 of the cash value. A policy loan balance, if any, will not be credited with the full rate of current interest.

Amounts shown (will change) (due to changes) in: current interest rate, cost of insurance rate, face amount, payment of premiums, death benefit option.

It is unlikely that dividends will be paid on this policy. Dividends, if any, will be small and paid only in later policy years.

Plan Design Summary: 10.00% Basis

End of Year	Total Premium	Cash Values	Difference	Death Benefit
5	5,040.00	3,815	1,224.73	100,000
10	10,080.00	10,857	-777.27	100,000
15	15,120.00	21,815	-6,694.62	100,000
20	20,160.00	39,048	-18,888.43	100,000
Age 65	30,240.00	112,275	-82,034.93	130,239
Mature 95	45,360.00	1,804,161	-1,758,801.49	1,894,370

Indexes Based on 5% Interest Rate

	10.00% Basis		4.50% Basis	
	10 Year	20 Year	10 Year	20 Year
Life Insurance Surrender Cost Index	1.86	-1.17	4.96	6.19
Life Insurance Net Payment Cost Index	10.08	10.08	10.08	10.08

New England Mutual Life Insurance Company

131

Life Insurance: Its Rate of Return

HOW TO CALCULATE THE BENEFICIARY'S RATE OF RETURN FOR ADJUSTABLE PREMIUM WHOLE LIFE (UNIVERSAL LIFE), OPTION B

Present value payment (premium) is $1,008 each and every year. Future value (the death benefit) is $100,000 plus the cash value. The cash value amount depends upon the interest assumption of 10%. The time span is the number of years you wish to measure.

Program: MONEY

One (1) Year Measurement

ON — XEQ — ALPHA — SIZE — ALPHA - 015
XEQ — ALPHA — MONEY — ALPHA
CLR ? R/S
END ? N R/S
BEGIN READY

1,008	CHS PMT
1	N
100,029	FV
I	Now calculating.
I =	9,823.51%
I =	Rate of Return

CLEAR DISPLAY. You must reenter program.

Calculate the Rate of Return for Life Insurance

Five (5) Year Measurement

ON — XEQ — ALPHA — SIZE — ALPHA — 015
XEQ — ALPHA — MONEY — ALPHA
CLR ?   R/S
END ?   N   R/S
BEGIN   READY

        1,008   CHS   PMT
           5   N
    103,795   FV
          I   Now calculating.
          I   =   125.50%
          I   =   Rate of Return

CLEAR DISPLAY. You must reenter program.

Fifteen (15) Year Measurement

ON — XEQ — ALPHA — SIZE — ALPHA — 015
XEQ — ALPHA — MONEY — ALPHA
CLR ?   R/S
END ?   N   R/S
BEGIN   READY

        1,008   CHS   PMT
          15   N
    121,250   FV
          I   Now calculating.
          I   =   23.58%
          I   =   Rate of Return

CLEAR DISPLAY. You must reenter program.

Life Insurance: Its Rate of Return

Thirty (30) Year Measurement

ON — XEQ — ALPHA — SIZE — ALPHA — 015
XEQ — ALPHA — MONEY — ALPHA
CLR ?   R/S
END ?   N   R/S
BEGIN   READY

```
           1,008     CHS   PMT
              30     N
         198,344    FV
               I    Now calculating.
               I  = 10.42%
               I  = Rate of Return
```

CLEAR DISPLAY. You must reenter program.

Forty-five (45) Year Measurement

ON — XEQ — ALPHA — SIZE — ALPHA — 015
XEQ — ALPHA — MONEY — ALPHA
CLR ?   R/S
END ?   N   R/S
BEGIN   READY

```
           1,008     CHS   PMT
              45     N
         458,507    FV
               I    Now calculating.
               I  = 8.27%
               I  = Rate of Return
```

CLEAR DISPLAY.

Calculate the Rate of Return for Life Insurance

HOW TO CALCULATE THE INSURED'S RATE OF RETURN FOR ADJUSTABLE PREMIUM WHOLE LIFE (UNIVERSAL LIFE), OPTION B

Note: You calculate the insured's rate of return in the exact manner as the beneficiary's rate of return. However, there is a different future value amount for the insured.

One (1) Year Measurement

ON — XEQ — ALPHA — SIZE — ALPHA — 015
XEQ — ALPHA — MONEY — ALPHA
CLR ?   R/S
END ?   N   R/S
BEGIN   READY

                1,008   CHS   PMT
                    1   N
                  34   FV
                   I   Now calculating.
                 I = 96.63%
                 I = Rate of Return

CLEAR DISPLAY. You must reenter program.

Life Insurance: Its Rate of Return

Five (5) Year Measurement

ON — XEQ — ALPHA — SIZE — ALPHA — 015
XEQ — ALPHA — MONEY — ALPHA
CLR ?   R/S
END ?   N   R/S
BEGIN   READY

        1,008   CHS   PMT
           5   N
        3,795   FV
           I   Now calculating.
           I = −9.31%
           I = Rate of Return

CLEAR DISPLAY. You must reenter program.

Fifteen (15) Year Measurement

ON — XEQ — ALPHA — SIZE — ALPHA — 015
XEQ — ALPHA — MONEY — ALPHA
CLR ?   R/S
END ?   N   R/S
BEGIN   READY

        1,008   CHS   PMT
          15   N
      21,250   FV
           I   Now calculating.
           I = 4.15%
           I = Rate of Return

CLEAR DISPLAY. You must reenter program.

Calculate the Rate of Return for Life Insurance

Thirty (30) Year Measurement

ON — XEQ — ALPHA — SIZE — ALPHA — 015
XEQ — ALPHA — MONEY — ALPHA
CLR ?   R/S
END ?   N   R/S
BEGIN   READY

      1,008   CHS   PMT
         30   N
    98,344   FV
          I   Now calculating.
          I   =   6.81%
          I   =   Rate of Return

CLEAR DISPLAY. You must reenter program.

Forty-five (45) Year Measurement

ON — XEQ — ALPHA — SIZE — ALPHA — 015
XEQ — ALPHA — MONEY — ALPHA
CLR ?   R/S
END ?   N   R/S
BEGIN   READY

     1,008   CHS   PMT
        45   N
   358,507   FV
         I   Now calculating.
         I   =   7.49%
         I   =   Rate of Return

CLEAR DISPLAY.

Life Insurance: Its Rate of Return

Plan: FLEXIBLE PREMIUM ADJUSTABLE LIFE
Issue Age: 35 MALE
Class: PREFERRED

Initial Face Amount: $100,000

Year	Age	Annual Premium	10.00% Basis (current) Cash Value	10.00% Basis (current) Death Benefit	4.50% Basis (guaranteed) Cash Value	4.50% Basis (guaranteed) Death Benefit
1	35	1,008.00	34	100,034	29	100,029
2	36	1,008.00	857	100,857	731	100,731
3	37	1,008.00	1,754	101,754	1,451	101,451
4	38	1,008.00	2,730	102,730	2,179	102,179
5	39	1,008.00	3,795	103,795	2,916	102,916
6	40	1,008.00	4,953	104,953	3,661	103,661
7	41	1,008.00	6,215	106,215	4,403	104,403
8	42	1,008.00	7,591	107,591	5,142	105,142
9	43	1,008.00	9,088	109,088	5,877	105,877
10	44	1,008.00	10,716	110,716	6,609	106,609
11	45	1,008.00	12,488	112,488	7,324	107,324
12	46	1,008.00	14,412	114,412	8,023	108,023
13	47	1,008.00	16,503	116,503	8,704	108,704
14	48	1,008.00	18,779	118,779	9,355	109,355
15	49	1,008.00	21,250	121,250	9,974	109,974
16	50	1,008.00	23,934	123,934	10,535	110,535
17	51	1,008.00	26,852	126,852	11,048	111,048
18	52	1,008.00	30,024	130,024	11,498	111,498
19	53	1,008.00	33,469	133,469	11,871	111,871
20	54	1,008.00	37,218	137,218	12,163	112,163
21	55	1,008.00	41,297	141,297	12,357	112,357

138

Calculate the Rate of Return for Life Insurance

22	56	1,008.00	45,735	12,438	112,438
23	57	1,008.00	50,563	12,376	112,376
24	58	1,008.00	55,814	12,164	112,164
25	59	1,008.00	61,521	11,783	111,783
26	60	1,008.00	67,727	11,202	111,202
27	61	1,008.00	74,469	10,398	110,398
28	62	1,008.00	81,789	9,350	109,350
29	63	1,008.00	89,730	8,035	108,035
30	64	1,008.00	98,344	6,403	106,403
31	65	1,008.00	107,681	4,416	104,416
32	66	1,008.00	117,796	2,033	102,033
33	67	1,008.00	128,757	**LAPSE	**LAPSE
34	68	1,008.00	140,633	0	0
35	69	1,008.00	153,500	0	0
36	70	1,008.00	167,442	0	0
37	71	1,008.00	182,555	0	0
38	72	1,008.00	198,936	0	0
39	73	1,008.00	216,698	0	0
40	74	1,008.00	235,954	0	0
45	79	1,008.00	358,507	0	0
50	84	0.00	525,022	0	0
55	89	0.00	750,417	0	0
60	94	0.00	1,074,412	0	0

			145,735	
			150,563	
			155,814	
			161,521	
			167,727	
			174,469	
			181,789	
			189,730	
			198,344	
			207,681	
			217,796	
			228,757	
			240,633	
			253,500	
			267,442	
			282,555	
			298,936	
			316,698	
			335,954	
			458,507	
			625,022	
			850,417	
			1,174,412	

**The policy will terminate at this time unless the plan premium is increased.

Life Insurance: Its Rate of Return

Current interest is credited on cash value over $500. Guaranteed interest is credited on the first $500 of the cash value. A policy loan balance, if any, will not be credited with the full rate of current interest.

Amounts shown (will change) (due to changes) in: current interest rate, cost of insurance rate, face amount, payment of premiums, death benefit option.

It is unlikely that dividends will be paid on this policy. Dividends, if any, will be small and paid only in later policy years.

Plan Design Summary: 10.00% Basis

End of Year	Total Premium	Cash Values	Difference	Death Benefits
5	5,040.00	3,795	1,245.15	103,795
10	10,080.00	10,716	-635.98	110,716
15	15,120.00	21,250	-6,130.12	121,250
20	20,160.00	37,218	-17,057.73	137,218
Age 65	30,240.00	98,344	-68,103.77	198,344
Mature 95	45,360.00	1,074,412	-1,029,052.17	1,174,412

Indexes Based on 5% Interest Rate

	10.00% Basis 10 Year	10.00% Basis 20 Year	4.50% Basis 10 Year	4.50% Basis 20 Year
Life Insurance Surrender Cost Index	1.90	-0.58	4.96	6.26
Life Insurance Net Payment Cost Index	9.76	9.20	9.85	9.60

New England Mutual Life Insurance Company

Calculate the Rate of Return for Life Insurance

HOW TO CALCULATE THE BENEFICIARY'S RATE OF RETURN FOR VARIABLE LIFE

Present value payment (premium) of $1,661.00 remains the same each and every year. Future value (the death benefit) is guaranteed to be not less than $100,000. If current interest rate assumption of 12% is achieved, the death benefit will increase. For this calculation, a 12% interest rate assumption is used. Time span is the number of years you wish to measure.

Program: MONEY

One (1) Year Measurement

ON — XEQ — ALPHA — SIZE — ALPHA — 015
XEQ — ALPHA — MONEY — ALPHA
CLR ?   R/S
END ?   N   R/S
BEGIN   READY

```
          102,924    FV
            1,661    CHS  PMT
                1    N
                I    Now calculating.
                I  = 6,096.51%
                I  = Rate of Return
```

CLEAR DISPLAY. You must reenter program.

Life Insurance: Its Rate of Return

Five (5) Year Measurement

ON — XEQ — ALPHA — SIZE — ALPHA — 015
XEQ — ALPHA — MONEY — ALPHA
CLR ?   R/S
End ?   N   R/S
BEGIN   READY

        116,747   FV
          1,661   CHS   PMT
             5   N
             I   Now calculating.
             I   =   106.10%
             I   =   Rate of Return

CLEAR DISPLAY. You must reenter program.

Fifteen (15) Year Measurement

ON — XEQ — ALPHA — SIZE — ALPHA — 015
XEQ — ALPHA — MONEY — ALPHA
CLR ?   R/S
END ?   N   R/S
BEGIN   READY

        175,865   FV
          1,661   CHS   PMT
            15   N
             I   Now calculating.
             I   =   22.20%
             I   =   Rate of Return

CLEAR DISPLAY. You must reenter program.

Calculate the Rate of Return for Life Insurance

Thirty (30) Year Measurement

ON — XEQ — ALPHA — SIZE — ALPHA — 015
XEQ — ALPHA — MONEY — ALPHA
CLR ?   R/S
END ?   N   R/S
BEGIN   READY

```
     383,896      FV
       1,661      CHS   PMT
          30      N
           I      Now calculating.
           I   =  11.22%
           I   =  Rate of Return
```

CLEAR DISPLAY. You must reenter program.

Thirty-five (35) Year Measurement

ON — XEQ — ALPHA — SIZE — ALPHA — 015
XEQ — ALPHA — MONEY — ALPHA
CLR ?   R/S
END ?   N   R/S
BEGIN   READY

```
     516,869      FV
       1,661      CHS   PMT
          35      N
           I      Now calculating.
           I   =  10.18%
           I   =  Rate of Return
```

CLEAR DISPLAY.

143

Life Insurance: Its Rate of Return

HOW TO CALCULATE THE INSURED'S RATE OF RETURN FOR VARIABLE LIFE

Note: You calculate the insured's rate of return in the exact manner as the beneficiary's rate of return. However, there is a different future value amount for the insured.

Program: MONEY

One (1) Year Measurement

ON — XEQ — ALPHA — SIZE — ALPHA — 015
XEQ — ALPHA — MONEY — ALPHA
CLR ?   R/S
END ?   N   R/S
BEGIN   READY

	1,661	CHS	PMT
	1	N	
	694	FV	
	I	Now calculating.	
	I =	−58.22%	
	I =	Rate of Return	

CLEAR DISPLAY. You must reenter program.

144

Calculate the Rate of Return for Life Insurance

Five (5) Year Measurement

ON — XEQ — ALPHA — SIZE — ALPHA — 015
XEQ — ALPHA — MONEY — ALPHA
CLR ?   R/S
END ?   N   R/S
BEGIN   READY

        1,661   CHS   PMT
           5   N
        7,233   FV
           I   Now calculating.
           I = −4.57%
           I = Rate of Return

CLEAR DISPLAY. You must reenter program.

Fifteen (15) Year Measurement

ON — XEQ — ALPHA — SIZE — ALPHA — 015
XEQ — ALPHA — MONEY — ALPHA
CLR ?   R/S
END ?   N   R/S
BEGIN   READY

        1,661   CHS   PMT
          15   N
     39,893   FV
           I   Now calculating.
           I = 5.69%
           I = Rate of Return

CLEAR DISPLAY. You must reenter program.

Life Insurance: Its Rate of Return

Thirty (30) Year Measurement

ON — XEQ — ALPHA — SIZE — ALPHA — 015
XEQ — ALPHA — MONEY — ALPHA
CLR ?   R/S
END ?   N   R/S
BEGIN   READY

1,661	CHS PMT
30	N
196,581	FV
I	Now calculating.
I =	7.83%
I =	Rate of Return

CLEAR DISPLAY. You must reenter program.

Thirty-five (35) Year Measurement

ON — XEQ — ALPHA — SIZE — ALPHA — 015
XEQ — ALPHA — MONEY — ALPHA
CLR ?   R/S
END ?   N   R/S
BEGIN   READY

1,661	CHS PMT
35	N
311,262	FV
I	Now calculating.
I =	8.03%
I =	Rate of Return

CLEAR DISPLAY.

Calculate the Rate of Return for Life Insurance

VARIABLE LIFE LEDGER STATEMENT

Plan: VARIABLE WHOLE LIFE 100
Issue Age: 35 MALE

Minimum Death Benefit: $100,000
Annual Premium: $1661.00*

Year	Premiums Accumulate At 5% Annum	0% Death Benefit Base Policy	0% Var PU Adds	0% Total	6% Death Benefit Base Policy	6% Var PU Adds	6% Total	12% Death Benefit Base Policy	12% Var PU Adds	12% Total
1	1,744	100,000	0	100,000	100,510	0	100,510	102,924	0	102,924
2	3,575	100,000	125	100,125	100,912	138	101,050	105,307	152	105,459
3	5,498	100,000	254	100,254	101,449	294	101,743	108,569	341	108,910
4	7,517	100,000	392	100,392	102,012	477	102,489	112,111	577	112,688
5	9,637	100,000	532	100,532	102,590	685	103,275	115,880	867	116,747
6	11,863	100,000	686	100,686	103,181	924	104,105	119,869	1,216	121,085
7	14,200	100,000	848	100,848	103,782	1,195	104,977	124,083	1,638	125,721
8	16,654	100,000	1,018	101,018	104,394	1,496	105,890	128,532	2,138	130,670
9	19,231	100,000	1,202	101,202	105,016	1,835	106,851	133,226	2,727	135,953
10	21,936	100,000	1,390	101,390	105,648	2,211	107,859	138,179	3,412	141,591
15	37,634	100,000	2,340	102,340	108,959	4,511	113,470	167,353	8,512	175,865
20	57,669	100,000	3,327	103,327	112,510	7,672	120,182	205,501	17,699	223,200
25	83,238	100,000	4,648	104,648	116,292	12,308	128,600	255,414	34,317	289,731
Age 65	115,873	100,000	6,097	106,097	120,292	18,608	138,900	320,746	63,150	383,896
35	157,523	100,000	7,358	107,358	124,488	26,374	150,862	406,239	110,630	516,869

147

Life Insurance: Its Rate of Return

Year	Premiums Accumulate At 5% Annum	0% Base Policy	0% Cash Value Var PU Adds	0% Total	6% Base Policy	6% Cash Value Var PU Adds	6% Total	12% Base Policy	12% Cash Value Var PU Adds	12% Total
1	1,744	661	0	661	678	0	678	694	0	694
2	3,575	1,884	36	1,920	1,969	40	2,009	2,055	44	2,099
3	5,498	3,090	76	3,166	3,314	88	3,402	3,546	102	3,648
4	7,517	4,277	121	4,398	4,710	147	4,857	5,177	178	5,355
5	9,637	5,444	169	5,613	6,159	218	6,377	6,957	276	7,233
6	11,863	6,589	225	6,814	7,659	304	7,963	8,898	400	9,298
7	14,200	7,711	288	7,999	9,211	405	9,616	11,013	556	11,569
8	16,654	8,811	356	9,167	10,816	524	11,340	13,317	748	14,065
9	19,231	9,887	434	10,321	12,476	662	13,138	15,827	984	16,811
10	21,936	10,940	517	11,457	14,190	823	15,013	18,559	1,270	19,829
15	37,634	15,827	1,010	16,837	23,581	1,948	25,529	36,218	3,675	39,893
20	57,669	20,011	1,649	21,660	34,266	3,803	38,069	62,588	8,773	71,361
25	83,238	23,448	2,614	26,062	46,113	6,922	53,035	101,278	19,299	120,577
Age 65	115,873	26,092	3,837	29,929	58,818	11,712	70,530	156,834	39,747	196,581
35	157,523	27,913	5,103	33,016	71,872	18,290	90,162	234,540	76,722	311,262

*Corresponding to Modal Premiums of: SEMI-ANNUAL $850.91 QUARTERLY $434.24 SPECIAL MONTHLY $144.08

Dividends illustrated are based on current scales and experience and are not guaranteed. It is emphasized that hypothetical investment results are illustrative only and should not be deemed representative of past or future investment results. Illustrations assume no policy loan has been made. This illustration must be preceded or accompanied by a current prospectus.

John Hancock Variable Life Insurance Company

12

HOW TO CALCULATE THE RATE OF RETURN FOR METHODS OF PREMIUM PAYMENT

Life Insurance: Its Rate of Return

HOW TO CALCULATE THE BENEFICIARY'S RATE OF RETURN FOR WHOLE LIFE (ORDINARY LIFE) METHOD OF PREMIUM PAYMENT

Tax-Qualified Minimum Deposit
(Direct Recognition Basis Used)

Here is a series of unequal present value payments (after tax outlay). Future value (the death benefit) changes each and every year. Time span is the number of years you wish to measure.

Note: Some years have a "no cost" outlay because of the tax savings.
Do not use "CHS" after the dollar amount in those years.

Program: MONEY

One (1) Year Measurement

ON — XEQ — ALPHA — SIZE — ALPHA — 015
XEQ — ALPHA — MONEY — ALPHA
CLR ?   R/S
END ?   R/S
BEGIN   READY

```
         1,301      CHS  PMT
             1      N
       100,000      FV
             |      Now calculating.
             | =    7,586.40%
             | =    Rate of Return
```

CLEAR DISPLAY. You now change programs.

150

Calculate the Rate of Return for Premium Payment

Program: IRR

Five (5) Year Measurement

ON — XEQ — ALPHA — SIZE — ALPHA — 023
XEQ — ALPHA — IRR — ALPHA
CLR ?   R/S
GROUPS ?   N   R/S
TOTL CFS = ?   6   R/S

CF 1	CF AMT = ?	1,301	CHS	R/S
CF 2	CF AMT = ?	1,243	CHS	R/S
CF 3	CF AMT = ?	0		R/S
CF 4	CF AMT = ?	48	CHS	R/S
CF 5	CF AMT = ?	94	CHS	R/S
CF 6	CF AMT = ?	101,521		R/S

CF CHANGES ?   N   R/S
Now calculating — will take a few minutes.

IRR = 122.44%   IRR = Rate of Return

CF 6 is the 5th-year net death benefit.

CLEAR DISPLAY. You must reenter program.

Life Insurance: Its Rate of Return

Fifteen (15) Year Measurement

ON — XEQ — ALPHA — SIZE — ALPHA — 033
XEQ — ALPHA — IRR — ALPHA
CLR ?   R/S
GROUPS ?   N   R/S
TOTL CFS = ?   16   R/S

CF 1	CF AMT = ?	1,301	CHS	R/S
CF 2	CF AMT = ?	1,243	CHS	R/S
CF 3	CF AMT = ?	0		R/S
CF 4	CF AMT = ?	48	CHS	R/S
CF 5	CF AMT = ?	94	CHS	R/S
CF 6	CF AMT = ?	1,238	CHS	R/S
CF 7	CF AMT = ?	1,169	CHS	R/S
CF 8	CF AMT = ?	3,853		R/S
CF 9	CF AMT = ?	39	CHS	R/S
CF 10	CF AMT = ?	26	CHS	R/S
CF 11	CF AMT = ?	13	CHS	R/S
CF 12	CF AMT = ?	1	CHS	R/S
CF 13	CF AMT = ?	7		R/S
CF 14	CF AMT = ?	27		R/S
CF 15	CF AMT = ?	46		R/S
CF 16	CF AMT = ?	101,475		R/S

CF CHANGES ?   N   R/S
Now calculating — will take a few minutes.

IRR = 28.80%   IRR = Rate of Return

CF 16 is the 15th-year net death benefit.

CLEAR DISPLAY. You must reenter program.

Calculate the Rate of Return for Premium Payment

Thirty (30) Year Measurement

ON — XEQ — ALPHA — SIZE — ALPHA - 048
XEQ — ALPHA — IRR — ALPHA
CLR ?   R/S
GROUPS ?   N   R/S
TOTL CFS = ?   31   R/S

CF 1	CF AMT = ?	1,301	CHS	R/S
CF 2	CF AMT = ?	1,243	CHS	R/S
CF 3	CF AMT = ?	0		R/S
CF 4	CF AMT = ?	48	CHS	R/S
CF 5	CF AMT = ?	94	CHS	R/S
CF 6	CF AMT = ?	1,238	CHS	R/S
CF 7	CF AMT = ?	1,169	CHS	R/S
CF 8	CF AMT = ?	3,853		R/S
CF 9	CF AMT = ?	39	CHS	R/S
CF 10	CF AMT = ?	26	CHS	R/S
CF 11	CF AMT = ?	13	CHS	R/S
CF 12	CF AMT = ?	1	CHS	R/S
CF 13	CF AMT = ?	7		R/S
CF 14	CF AMT = ?	27		R/S
CF 15	CF AMT = ?	46		R/S
CF 16	CF AMT = ?	53		R/S
CF 17	CF AMT = ?	49		R/S
CF 18	CF AMT = ?	41		R/S
CF 19	CF AMT = ?	24		R/S
CF 20	CF AMT = ?	2		R/S
CF 21	CF AMT = ?	26	CHS	R/S
CF 22	CF AMT = ?	38	CHS	R/S
CF 23	CF AMT = ?	64	CHS	R/S
CF 24	CF AMT = ?	99	CHS	R/S
CF 25	CF AMT = ?	137	CHS	R/S
CF 26	CF AMT = ?	184	CHS	R/S
CF 27	CF AMT = ?	239	CHS	R/S
CF 28	CF AMT = ?	304	CHS	R/S
CF 29	CF AMT = ?	385	CHS	R/S
CF 30	CF AMT = ?	476	CHS	R/S
CF 31	CF AMT = ?	106,735		R/S

CF CHANGES ?   N   R/S
Now calculating — will take a few minutes.

IRR = 13.87%   IRR = Rate of Return

CF 31 is the 30th-year net death benefit.

CLEAR DISPLAY.

Life Insurance: Its Rate of Return

HOW TO CALCULATE THE INSURED'S RATE OF RETURN FOR WHOLE LIFE (ORDINARY LIFE) METHOD OF PREMIUM PAYMENT

Tax-Qualified Minimum Deposit
(Direct Recognition Basis Used)

Note: You calculate the insured's rate of return in the exact manner as the beneficiary's rate of return. However, use the net equity figure from the ledger statement for the insured's future value.

One (1) Year Measurement

It is not necessary to do this calculation as the future value to the insured is zero (0) and the rate of return is −100% compound.

Calculate the Rate of Return for Premium Payment

Program: IRR

Five (5) Year Measurement

ON — XEQ — ALPHA — SIZE — ALPHA — 023
XEQ — ALPHA — IRR — ALPHA
CLR ?   R/S
GROUPS ?   N   R/S
TOTL CFS = ?   6   R/S

CF 1	CF AMT = ?	1,301	CHS	R/S
CF 2	CF AMT = ?	1,243	CHS	R/S
CF 3	CF AMT = ?	0		R/S
CF 4	CF AMT = ?	48	CHS	R/S
CF 5	CF AMT = ?	94	CHS	R/S
CF 6	CF AMT = ?	1,521		R/S

CF CHANGES ?   N   R/S
Now calculating — will take a few minutes.

IRR = 12.42%   IRR = Rate of Return

CF 6 is the 5th-year net equity.

CLEAR DISPLAY. You must reenter program.

Life Insurance: Its Rate of Return

Fifteen (15) Year Measurement

ON — XEQ — ALPHA — SIZE — ALPHA — 033
XEQ — ALPHA — IRR — ALPHA
CLR ?   R/S
GROUPS ?   N   R/S
TOTL CFS = ?   16   R/S

CF 1	CF AMT = ?	1,301	CHS	R/S
CF 2	CF AMT = ?	1,243	CHS	R/S
CF 3	CF AMT = ?	0		R/S
CF 4	CF AMT = ?	48	CHS	R/S
CF 5	CF AMT = ?	94	CHS	R/S
CF 6	CF AMT = ?	1,238	CHS	R/S
CF 7	CF AMT = ?	1,169	CHS	R/S
CF 8	CF AMT = ?	3,853	CHS	R/S
CF 9	CF AMT = ?	39	CHS	R/S
CF 10	CF AMT = ?	26	CHS	R/S
CF 11	CF AMT = ?	13	CHS	R/S
CF 12	CF AMT = ?	1	CHS	R/S
CF 13	CF AMT = ?	7		R/S
CF 14	CF AMT = ?	27		R/S
CF 15	CF AMT = ?	46		R/S
CF 16	CF AMT = ?	1,475		R/S

CF CHANGES ?   N   R/S
Now calculating — will take a few minutes.

IRR = 0.72%   IRR = Rate of Return

CF 16 is the 15th-year net equity.

CLEAR DISPLAY. You must reenter program.

Calculate the Rate of Return for Premium Payment

Thirty (30) Year Measurement

ON — XEQ — ALPHA — SIZE — ALPHA - 048
XEQ — ALPHA — IRR — ALPHA
CLR ?   R/S
GROUPS ?   N   R/S
TOTL CFS = ?   31   R/S

CF 1	CF AMT = ?	1,301	CHS	R/S
CF 2	CF AMT = ?	1,243	CHS	R/S
CF 3	CF AMT = ?	0		R/S
CF 4	CF AMT = ?	48	CHS	R/S
CF 5	CF AMT = ?	94	CHS	R/S
CF 6	CF AMT = ?	1,238	CHS	R/S
CF 7	CF AMT = ?	1,169	CHS	R/S
CF 8	CF AMT = ?	3,853	CHS	R/S
CF 9	CF AMT = ?	39	CHS	R/S
CF 10	CF AMT = ?	26	CHS	R/S
CF 11	CF AMT = ?	13	CHS	R/S
CF 12	CF AMT = ?	1	CHS	R/S
CF 13	CF AMT = ?	7		R/S
CF 14	CF AMT = ?	27		R/S
CF 15	CF AMT = ?	46		R/S
CF 16	CF AMT = ?	53		R/S
CF 17	CF AMT = ?	49		R/S
CF 18	CF AMT = ?	41		R/S
CF 19	CF AMT = ?	24		R/S
CF 20	CF AMT = ?	2		R/S
CF 21	CF AMT = ?	26	CHS	R/S
CF 22	CF AMT = ?	38	CHS	R/S
CF 23	CF AMT = ?	64	CHS	R/S
CF 24	CF AMT = ?	99	CHS	R/S
CF 25	CF AMT = ?	137	CHS	R/S
CF 26	CF AMT = ?	184	CHS	R/S
CF 27	CF AMT = ?	239	CHS	R/S
CF 28	CF AMT = ?	304	CHS	R/S
CF 29	CF AMT = ?	385	CHS	R/S
CF 30	CF AMT = ?	476	CHS	R/S
CF 31	CF AMT = ?	3,471		R/S

CF CHANGES ?   N   R/S
Now calculating — will take a few minutes.

IRR = 0.74%   IRR = Rate of Return

CF 31 is the 30th-year net equity.

CLEAR DISPLAY.

Life Insurance: Its Rate of Return

FLEXIBLE PAYMENT ILLUSTRATION

Plan: ORDINARY LIFE+
Issue Age: 35 MALE
Class: PREFERRED STANDARD
Loan Interest Rate: 8%

Annual Premium: $1,301.00
Face Amount: $100,000

Policy Year	Cash Value	Cost of One-Year Term*	Net Annual Premium	Annual Loan Increase	Total Loan	Annual Loan Interest	Annual Cash Outlay*	Net Death Benefit*
1	0	0	1301	0	0	0	1301	100000
2	1215	1	1243	0	0	0	1243	101215
3	2438	2	1185	1185	1185	0	0	101253
4	3699	4	1159	1159	2345	95	95	101354
5	4997	6	1131	1131	3476	188	188	101521
Total		13	6019			283	2827	
6	6330	8	1099	0	3476	278	1377	102854
7	7699	10	1030	0	3476	278	1308	104223
8	9104	13	960	4954	8430	278	3715–	100674
9	10545	17	1037	1334	9764	674	376	100781
10	12022	21	1003	1368	11131	781	416	100891
Total		82	11148			2572	2589	
11	13534	26	968	1400	12531	891	458	101003
12	15081	32	932	1432	13964	1103	502	101117
13	16660	40	897	1462	15426	1117	551	101234
14	18271	49	847	1492	16918	1234	589	101353
15	19912	60	796	1519	18437	1353	630	101475
Total		289	15588			8170	5319	

158

Calculate the Rate of Return for Premium Payment

16	21581	73	755	1545	19982	1475	684	101848
17	23276	87	722	1569	21552	1599	750	102253
18	24997	104	690	1594	23145	1724	820	102702
19	26742	124	665	1616	24761	1852	901	103193
20	28509	147	643	1636	26397	1981	988	103730
Total		824	19063			16801	9462	
21	30297	172	626	1656	28053	2122	1082	104311
22	32103	202	589	1672	29725	2244	1160	104575
23	33925	236	563	1687	31412	2378	1253	104840
24	35759	275	540	1698	33110	2513	1355	105109
25	37603	319	520	1707	34818	2649	1461	105378
Total		2028	21901			28697	15773	
26	39454	369	505	1714	36531	2785	1576	105649
27	41308	425	494	1717	38248	2923	1700	105920
28	43163	491	493	1718	39966	3060	1834	106192
29	45016	566	502	1716	41681	3197	1983	106464
30	46863	650	519	1710	43392	3335	2143	106735
Total		4529	24414			43997	25009	

Dividends* used to purchase One-Year Term Insurance with balance to reduce premiums. Excess dividends, if any, are illustrated first as reducing the loan and next as a negative annual cash outlay. Total loan will not exceed 92% of the policy cash value. Illustrated dividends have been reduced due to the projected policy loans.

New England Mutual Life Insurance Company

Life Insurance: Its Rate of Return

FLEXIBLE PAYMENT ILLUSTRATION
Tax Statement

Policy Year	Pre-Tax Annual Cash Outlay	Annual Loan Interest	Assumed Tax Bracket	Assumed Tax Savings*	After-Tax Outlay*	Net Equity*
1	1301	0	50	0	1301	0
2	1243	0	50	0	1243	1215
3	0	0	50	0	0	1253
4	95	95	50	48	48	1354
5	188	188	50	94	94	1521
Total	2827	283				
6	1377	278	50	139	1238	2854
7	1308	278	50	139	1169	4223
8	3715–	278	50	139	3853–	674
9	376	674	50	337	39	781
10	416	781	50	391	26	891
Total	2589	2572				
11	458	891	50	446	13	1003
12	502	1003	50	502	1	1117
13	551	1117	50	559	7–	1234
14	589	1234	50	617	27–	1353
15	630	1353	50	677	46–	1475
Total	5319	8170				

160

Calculate the Rate of Return for Premium Payment

16	684	1475	50	738	1599
17	750	1599	50	800	1724
18	820	1724	50	862	1852
19	901	1852	50	926	1981
20	988	1981	50	991	2112
Total	9462	16801			
21	1082	2112	50	1056	2244
22	1160	2244	50	1122	2378
23	1253	2378	50	1189	2513
24	1355	2513	50	1257	2649
25	1461	2649	50	1325	2785
Total	15773	28697			
26	1576	2785	50	1393	2923
27	1700	2923	50	1462	3060
28	1834	3060	50	1530	3197
29	1983	3197	50	1599	3335
30	2143	3335	50	1668	3471
Total	25009	43997			

53–	
49–	
41–	
24–	
2–	
26	
38	
64	
99	
137	
184	
239	
304	
385	
476	

Each net equity figure shown above equals the total cash value, less the total loan, after payment of the annual premium. The tax savings, which are included in the Policy Year 30 totals, are based on the following tax brackets and durations:

Brackets: 50%
Years: 1–65

New England Mutual Life Insurance Company

161

Life Insurance: Its Rate of Return

Time Period	Pre-Tax Total Cash Outlay*	Assumed Tax Savings*	After-Tax Outlay**	Net Equity*	After-Tax Outlay Less Net Equity*
5 Years	3105	281	2824	1730	1094
10 Years	3480	1733	1747	1250	497
15 Years	6794	4826	1968	2342	374–
20 Years	11574	9461	2113	5026	2913–
Age 65	28480	23742	4738	8368	3630–

Summary figures are end of year values. Pre-Tax Outlay assumes cash payment of any interest due in the final year of the time period. An adjustment for that interest is made in the tax savings and After-Tax Outlay figures. Net Equity is the amount from the tax statement plus any dividends payable.

Interest-Adjusted* Indexes based on a 5.00% interest rate, for basic policy only:

Life Insurance Net Payment Cost Index	10 yrs: $10.94	20 yrs: $ 9.51	Age 65: $ 8.06
Life Insurance Surrender Cost Index	10 yrs: $ 1.84	20 yrs: $ 0.71	Age 65: $ 0.85
Equivalent Level Annual Dividend	10 yrs: $ 2.07	20 yrs: $ 3.50	Age 65: $ 4.95

NOTE: Whenever the total loan exceeds the death benefit provided by any dividend values and any One-Year Term Insurance, the Net Death Benefit* will be less than the face amount of the policy. Based on the 1983 dividend scale and One-Year Term rates, this will occur in policy year 43. Thereafter, the Net Death Benefit will usually remain below the face amount, unless the difference is offset by either a decrease in the amount of borrowing or an increase in loan repayment.

Calculate the Rate of Return for Premium Payment

Policy Year	Cash Value	Cost Of One-Year Term*	Net Annual Premium	Annual Loan Increase	Total Loan	Annual Loan Interest	Annual Cash Outlay*	Net Death Benefit*
43	68778	2488	1301	1431	63683	4980	4849	98240
44	70283	2563	1301	1394	65077	5095	5002	93698
45	71736	2642	1301	1345	66422	5206	5161	88868
46	73135	2715	1301	1295	67718	5314	5319	83683
47	74477	2769	1301	1243	68960	5417	5475	78264
48	75767	2807	1301	1194	70155	5517	5623	72920

+ The values shown in the ledger assume an annual mode of premium payment and a(n) 8.00% fixed policy loan interest rate applied in arrears. The issuance of any policies or riders is subject to the Company's regular underwriting practices. The amounts of coverage and premiums for any policies or riders, if issued, may differ from those illustrated.

** Includes dividend values. Dividends are a return of part of the premium and primarily depend on investment earnings, mortality and expense experience. Dividends are computed on current dividend scale and are neither guarantees nor estimates for the future. A Terminal Dividend is payable upon surrender, lapse or death, after at least 15 policy years, but only if declared by the Company at such time, and is included in the Interest-Adjusted Surrender Cost Index.

Based on current dividend scale, dividends will be insufficient to purchase an amount of One-Year Term Insurance equal to the policy cash value in policy year 47 and usually thereafter. Premiums for One-Year Term Insurance are not guaranteed and are subject to change.

* Current law provides that loan interest may be tax-deductible provided certain requirements are met. This illustration assumes cash payment of any interest due during policy year 1-7. In any year thereafter, any interest in excess of annual cash outlay is assumed to be borrowed. For cash basis taxpayers, interest is deductible if paid in cash but not deductible if added to the policy loan. In the event the policy is surrendered, there may be a gain which is taxable as ordinary income. For specific tax information, consult your tax advisor.
New England Mutual Life Insurance Company

Life Insurance: Its Rate of Return

HOW TO CALCULATE THE BENEFICIARY'S RATE OF RETURN FOR WHOLE LIFE (ORDINARY LIFE) METHOD OF PREMIUM PAYMENT

Tax-Qualified Minimum Deposit
(Direct Recognition Basis Not Used)

Here is a series of unequal present value payments (after tax outlay). Future value (the death benefit) changes each and every year. Time span is the number of years you wish to measure.

Note: Some years have a "no cost" outlay because of the tax savings.

Do not use "CHS" after the dollar amount in those years.

Program: MONEY

One (1) Year Measurement

ON — XEQ — ALPHA — SIZE — ALPHA — 015
XEQ — ALPHA — MONEY — ALPHA
CLR ?   R/S
END ?   R/S
BEGIN   READY

1,582	CHS PMT	
1	N	
100,000	FV	
I	Now calculating.	
I =	6,221.11%	
I =	Rate of Return	

CLEAR DISPLAY. You now change programs.

164

Calculate the Rate of Return for Premium Payment

Program: IRR

Five (5) Year Measurement

ON — XEQ — ALPHA — SIZE — ALPHA — 023
XEQ — ALPHA — IRR — ALPHA
CLR ?   R/S
GROUPS ?   N   R/S
TOTL CFS = ?   6   R/S

CF 1	CF AMT = ?	1,582	CHS	R/S
CF 2	CF AMT = ?	1,461	CHS	R/S
CF 3	CF AMT = ?	0		R/S
CF 4	CF AMT = ?	55	CHS	R/S
CF 5	CF AMT = ?	108	CHS	R/S
CF 6	CF AMT = ?	101,072		R/S

CF CHANGES ?   N   R/S
Now calculating — will take a few minutes.

IRR = 113.53%   IRR = Rate of Return

CF 6 is the 5th-year net death benefit.

CLEAR DISPLAY. You must reenter program.

Life Insurance: Its Rate of Return

Fifteen (15) Year Measurement

ON — XEQ — ALPHA — SIZE — ALPHA — 033
XEQ — ALPHA — IRR — ALPHA
CLR ?   R/S
GROUPS ?   N   R/S
TOTL CFS = ?   16   R/S

CF 1	CF AMT = ?	1,582	CHS	R/S
CF 2	CF AMT = ?	1,461	CHS	R/S
CF 3	CF AMT = ?	0		R/S
CF 4	CF AMT = ?	55	CHS	R/S
CF 5	CF AMT = ?	108	CHS	R/S
CF 6	CF AMT = ?	1,299	CHS	R/S
CF 7	CF AMT = ?	1,220	CHS	R/S
CF 8	CF AMT = ?	3,844		R/S
CF 9	CF AMT = ?	232		R/S
CF 10	CF AMT = ?	284		R/S
CF 11	CF AMT = ?	243		R/S
CF 12	CF AMT = ?	288		R/S
CF 13	CF AMT = ?	328		R/S
CF 14	CF AMT = ?	383		R/S
CF 15	CF AMT = ?	439		R/S
CF 16	CF AMT = ?	101,566		R/S

CF CHANGES ?   N   R/S
Now calculating — will take a few minutes.

IRR = 27.65%   IRR = Rate of Return

CF 16 is the 15th-year net death benefit.

CLEAR DISPLAY. You must reenter program.

Calculate the Rate of Return for Premium Payment

Thirty (30) Year Measurement

ON — XEQ — ALPHA — SIZE — ALPHA - 048
XEQ — ALPHA — IRR — ALPHA
CLR ?   R/S
GROUPS ?   N   R/S
TOTL CFS = ?   31   R/S

CF 1	CF AMT = ?	1,582	CHS	R/S
CF 2	CF AMT = ?	1,461	CHS	R/S
CF 3	CF AMT = ?	0		R/S
CF 4	CF AMT = ?	55	CHS	R/S
CF 5	CF AMT = ?	108	CHS	R/S
CF 6	CF AMT = ?	1,299	CHS	R/S
CF 7	CF AMT = ?	1,220	CHS	R/S
CF 8	CF AMT = ?	3,844		R/S
CF 9	CF AMT = ?	232		R/S
CF 10	CF AMT = ?	284		R/S
CF 11	CF AMT = ?	243		R/S
CF 12	CF AMT = ?	288		R/S
CF 13	CF AMT = ?	328		R/S
CF 14	CF AMT = ?	383		R/S
CF 15	CF AMT = ?	439		R/S
CF 16	CF AMT = ?	486		R/S
CF 17	CF AMT = ?	525		R/S
CF 18	CF AMT = ?	560		R/S
CF 19	CF AMT = ?	592		R/S
CF 20	CF AMT = ?	615		R/S
CF 21	CF AMT = ?	637		R/S
CF 22	CF AMT = ?	666		R/S
CF 23	CF AMT = ?	684		R/S
CF 24	CF AMT = ?	695		R/S
CF 25	CF AMT = ?	701		R/S
CF 26	CF AMT = ?	698		R/S
CF 27	CF AMT = ?	692		R/S
CF 28	CF AMT = ?	669		R/S
CF 29	CF AMT = ?	635		R/S
CF 30	CF AMT = ?	591		R/S
CF 31	CF AMT = ?	105,261		R/S

CF CHANGES ?   N   R/S
Now calculating — will take a few minutes.

IRR = 14.78%   IRR = Rate of Return

CF 31 is the 30th-year net death benefit.

CLEAR DISPLAY.

Life Insurance: Its Rate of Return

HOW TO CALCULATE THE INSURED'S RATE OF RETURN FOR WHOLE LIFE (ORDINARY LIFE) METHOD OF PREMIUM PAYMENT

Tax-Qualified Minimum Deposit
(Direct Recognition Basis Not Used)

Note: You calculate the insured's rate of return in the exact manner as the beneficiary's rate of return. However, use the net equity figure from the ledger statement for the insured's future value.

One (1) Year Measurement

It is not necessary to do this calculation as the future value to the insured is zero (0) and the rate of return is –100% compound.

Calculate the Rate of Return for Premium Payment

Program: IRR

Five (5) Year Measurement

ON — XEQ — ALPHA — SIZE — ALPHA — 023
XEQ — ALPHA — IRR — ALPHA
CLR ?   R/S
GROUPS ?   N   R/S
TOTL CFS = ?   6   R/S

CF 1	CF AMT = ?	1,582	CHS	R/S
CF 2	CF AMT = ?	1,461	CHS	R/S
CF 3	CF AMT = ?	0		R/S
CF 4	CF AMT = ?	55	CHS	R/S
CF 5	CF AMT = ?	108	CHS	R/S
CF 6	CF AMT = ?	1,072		R/S

CF CHANGES ?   N   R/S
Now calculating — will take a few minutes.

IRR = −22.75%   IRR = Rate of Return

CF 6 is the 5th-year net equity.

CLEAR DISPLAY. You must reenter program.

Life Insurance: Its Rate of Return

Fifteen (15) Year Measurement

ON — XEQ — ALPHA — SIZE — ALPHA — 033
XEQ — ALPHA — IRR — ALPHA
CLR ?   R/S
GROUPS ?   N   R/S
TOTL CFS = ?   16   R/S

CF 1	CF AMT = ?	1,582	CHS	R/S
CF 2	CF AMT = ?	1,461	CHS	R/S
CF 3	CF AMT = ?	0		R/S
CF 4	CF AMT = ?	55	CHS	R/S
CF 5	CF AMT = ?	108	CHS	R/S
CF 6	CF AMT = ?	1,299	CHS	R/S
CF 7	CF AMT = ?	1,220	CHS	R/S
CF 8	CF AMT = ?	3,844		R/S
CF 9	CF AMT = ?	232		R/S
CF 10	CF AMT = ?	284		R/S
CF 11	CF AMT = ?	243		R/S
CF 12	CF AMT = ?	288		R/S
CF 13	CF AMT = ?	328		R/S
CF 14	CF AMT = ?	383		R/S
CF 15	CF AMT = ?	439		R/S
CF 16	CF AMT = ?	1,566		R/S

CF CHANGES ?   N   R/S
Now calculating — will take a few minutes.

IRR = 4.11%   IRR = Rate of Return

CF 16 is the 15th-year net equity.

CLEAR DISPLAY. You must reenter program.

Calculate the Rate of Return for Premium Payment

Thirty (30) Year Measurement

ON — XEQ — ALPHA — SIZE — ALPHA - 048
XEQ — ALPHA — IRR — ALPHA
CLR ?   R/S
GROUPS ?   N   R/S
TOTL CFS = ?   31   R/S

CF 1	CF AMT = ?	1,582	CHS	R/S
CF 2	CF AMT = ?	1,461	CHS	R/S
CF 3	CF AMT = ?	0		R/S
CF 4	CF AMT = ?	55	CHS	R/S
CF 5	CF AMT = ?	108	CHS	R/S
CF 6	CF AMT = ?	1,299	CHS	R/S
CF 7	CF AMT = ?	1,220	CHS	R/S
CF 8	CF AMT = ?	3,844		R/S
CF 9	CF AMT = ?	232		R/S
CF 10	CF AMT = ?	284		R/S
CF 11	CF AMT = ?	243		R/S
CF 12	CF AMT = ?	288		R/S
CF 13	CF AMT = ?	328		R/S
CF 14	CF AMT = ?	383		R/S
CF 15	CF AMT = ?	439		R/S
CF 16	CF AMT = ?	486		R/S
CF 17	CF AMT = ?	525		R/S
CF 18	CF AMT = ?	560		R/S
CF 19	CF AMT = ?	592		R/S
CF 20	CF AMT = ?	615		R/S
CF 21	CF AMT = ?	637		R/S
CF 22	CF AMT = ?	666		R/S
CF 23	CF AMT = ?	684		R/S
CF 24	CF AMT = ?	695		R/S
CF 25	CF AMT = ?	701		R/S
CF 26	CF AMT = ?	698		R/S
CF 27	CF AMT = ?	692		R/S
CF 28	CF AMT = ?	669		R/S
CF 29	CF AMT = ?	635		R/S
CF 30	CF AMT = ?	591		R/S
CF 31	CF AMT = ?	3,598		R/S

CF CHANGES ?   N   R/S
Now calculating — will take a few minutes.

IRR = 9.15%   IRR = Rate of Return

CF 31 is the 30th-year net equity.

CLEAR DISPLAY.

Life Insurance: Its Rate of Return

FLEXIBLE PAYMENT ILLUSTRATION

Plan: ORDINARY LIFE+
Issue Age: 35 MALE
Class: PREFERRED STANDARD
Loan Interest Rate: 8%

Annual Premium $1,582.00
Face Amount: $100,000

Policy Year	Cash Value	Cost of One-Year Term*	Net Annual Premium	Annual Loan Increase	Total Loan	Annual Loan Interest	Annual Cash Outlay*	Net Death Benefit*
1	0	0	1582	0	0	0	1582	100000
2	684	1	1461	0	0	0	1461	100684
3	2076	2	1381	1381	1381	0	0	100695
4	3507	4	1302	1302	2683	110	110	100824
5	4976	6	1222	1222	3904	215	215	101072
Total		13	6948			325	3368	
6	6481	8	1143	0	3904	312	1455	102577
7	8024	11	1064	0	3904	312	1376	104120
8	9603	14	986	4987	8892	312	3689–	100711
9	11219	18	909	1496	10388	711	123	100831
10	12872	22	831	1531	11919	831	131	100953
Total		86	11881			2803	2764	
11	14466	28	756	1476	13394	953	233	101072
12	16091	35	681	1505	14899	1072	247	101192
13	17746	43	608	1532	16431	1192	267	101315
14	19428	52	517	1557	17989	1315	274	101439
15	21136	63	422	1581	19570	1439	280	101566
Total		307	14865			8774	4065	

Calculate the Rate of Return for Premium Payment

16	22868	77	335	1604	21174	1566	296	101821
17	24623	92	252	1625	22799	1694	321	102080
18	26398	110	171	1644	24443	1824	351	102359
19	28194	131	93	1663	26106	1955	385	102658
20	30007	154	19	1679	27784	2088	428	102979
Total		871	15735			17901	5846	
21	31837	181	54–	1694	29479	2223	474	103318
22	33680	212	139–	1706	31185	2358	512	103527
23	35534	247	215–	1716	32902	2495	563	103737
24	37396	288	287–	1724	34626	2632	620	103950
25	39263	333	357–	1728	36355	2770	683	104165
Total		2132	14683			30379	8698	
26	41131	384	423–	1729	38084	2908	755	104382
27	42999	443	486–	1729	39814	3047	831	104600
28	44863	511	535–	1725	41540	3185	923	104819
29	46720	587	578–	1719	43259	3323	1026	105040
30	48567	673	611–	1710	44969	3461	1139	105261
Total		4730	12050			46303	13372	

Dividends* used to purchase One-Year Term Insurance with balance to reduce premiums. Excess dividends, if any, are illustrated first as reducing the loan and next as a negative annual cash outlay. Total loan will not exceed 92% of the policy cash value.

New England Mutual Life Insurance Company

FLEXIBLE PAYMENT ILLUSTRATION
Tax Statement

Policy Year	Pre-Tax Annual Cash Outlay	Annual Loan Interest	Assumed Tax Bracket	Assumed Tax Savings*	After-Tax Outlay**	Net Equity*
1	1582	0	50	0	1582	0
2	1461	0	50	0	1461	684
3	0	0	50	0	0	695
4	110	110	50	55	55	824
5	215	215	50	108	108	1072
Total	3368	325				
6	1455	312	50	156	1299	2577
7	1376	312	50	156	1220	4120
8	3689–	312	50	156	3844–	711
9	123	711	50	356	232–	831
10	131	831	50	416	284–	953
Total	2764	2803				
11	233	953	50	477	243–	1072
12	247	1072	50	536	288–	1192
13	267	1192	50	596	328–	1315
14	274	1315	50	658	383–	1439
15	280	1439	50	720	439–	1566
Total	4065	8774				

Calculate the Rate of Return for Premium Payment

16	296	1566	50	783	486–	1694
17	321	1694	50	847	525–	1824
18	351	1824	50	912	560–	1955
19	385	1955	50	978	592–	2088
20	428	2088	50	1044	615–	2223
Total	5846	17901				
21	474	2223	50	1112	637–	2358
22	512	2358	50	1179	666–	2495
23	563	2495	50	1248	684–	2632
24	620	2632	50	1316	695–	2770
25	683	2770	50	1385	701–	2908
Total	8698	30379				
26	755	2908	50	1454	698–	3047
27	831	3047	50	1524	692–	3185
28	923	3185	50	1593	669–	3323
29	1026	3323	50	1662	635–	3461
30	1139	3461	50	1731	591–	3598
Total	13372	46303				

Each net equity figure shown above equals the total cash value, less the total loan, after payment of the annual premium. The tax savings, which are included in the Policy Year 30 totals, are based on the following tax brackets and durations:

Brackets: 50%
Years: 1-65

New England Mutual Life Insurance Company

Life Insurance: Its Rate of Return

Time Period	Pre-Tax Total Cash Outlay*	Assumed Tax Savings*	After-Tax Outlay**	Net Equity*	After-Tax Outlay Less Net Equity*
5 Years	3680	319	3361	1519	1842
10 Years	3717	1880	1837	1807	30
15 Years	5631	5173	458	3017	2559–
20 Years	8069	10066	1997–	5000	6997–
Age 65	16970	24957	7987–	8331	16318–

Summary figures are end of year values. Pre-Tax Outlay assumes cash payment of any interest due in the final year of the time period. An adjustment for that interest is made in the Tax Savings and After-Tax Outlay figures. Net Equity is the amount from the tax statement plus any dividends payable.

Interest-Adjusted* Indexes based on a 5.00% interest rate, for basic policy only:

Life Insurance Net Payment Cost Index	10 yrs: 11.48	20 yrs: 8.31	Age 65: 5.39
Life Insurance Surrender Cost Index	10 yrs: 1.74	20 yrs: 0.61–	Age 65: 1.82–
Equivalent Level Annual Dividend	10 yrs: 4.34	20 yrs: 7.51	Age 65: 10.43

NOTE: Whenever the total loan exceeds the death benefit provided by any dividend values and any One-Year Term Insurance, the Net Death Benefit* will be less than the face amount of the policy. Based on the 1983 dividend scale and One-Year Term rates, this will occur in policy year 48. Thereafter, the Net Death Benefit will usually remain below the face amount, unless the difference is offset by either a decrease in the amount of borrowing or an increase in loan repayment.

Calculate the Rate of Return for Premium Payment

Policy Year	Cash Value	Cost Of One-Year Term*	Net Annual Premium	Annual Loan Increase	Total Loan	Annual Loan Interest	Annual Cash Outlay*	Net Death Benefit**
48	76954	4991	1582	1155	71254	5608	6035	99467
49	78154	5045	1582	1111	72365	5700	6171	91562
50	79315	5083	1582	1075	73440	5789	6296	84277
51	80444	5106	1582	1045	74485	5875	6411	77629
52	81547	5118	1582	1021	75506	5959	6519	71583
53	82635	5120	1582	1007	76514	6041	6615	66154

+ The values shown in the ledger assume an annual mode of premium payment and a(n) 8.00% fixed policy loan interest rate applied in arrears. The issuance of any policies or riders is subject to the Company's regular underwriting practices. The amounts of coverage and premiums for any policies or riders, if issued, may differ from those illustrated.

** Includes dividend values. Dividends are a return of part of the premium and primarily depend on investment earnings, mortality and expense experience. Dividends are computed on current dividend scale and are neither guarantees nor estimates for the future. A Terminal Dividend is payable upon surrender, lapse or death, after at least 15 policy years, but only if declared by the Company at such time, and is included in the Interest-Adjusted Surrender Cost Index.

Based on current dividend scale, dividends will be insufficient to purchase an amount of One-Year Term Insurance equal to the policy cash value in policy year 47 and usually thereafter.

Premiums for One-Year Term Insurance are not guaranteed and are subject to change.

* Current law provides that loan interest may be tax-deductible provided certain requirements are met. This illustration assumes cash payment of any interest due during policy year 1-7. In any year thereafter, any interest in excess of annual cash outlay is assumed to be borrowed. For cash basis taxpayers, interest is deductible if paid in cash but not deductible if added to the policy loan. In the event the policy is surrendered, there may be a gain which is taxable as ordinary income. For specific tax information, consult your tax advisor.

New England Mutual Life Insurance Company

177

Life Insurance: Its Rate of Return

HOW TO CALCULATE THE BENEFICIARY'S RATE OF RETURN FOR WHOLE LIFE (ORDINARY LIFE) METHOD OF PREMIUM PAYMENT

Premium Offset/Vanishing Premium

Here is a series of equal present value payments (premiums) of $1,301.00 each and every year for 9 years. From year 10 onward, there is zero (0) outlay each and every year. Future value (the total death benefit) changes each and every year. Time span is the number of years you wish to measure.

Program: IRR

One (1) Year Measurement

ON — XEQ — ALPHA — SIZE — ALPHA — 021
XEQ — ALPHA — IRR — ALPHA
CLR ?   R/S
GROUPS ?   R/S
TOTL GROUPS = ?   2   R/S
GROUP 1 CF AMT = ?   1,301   CHS   R/S
No. CFS = ?   1   R/S
GROUP 2 CF AMT = ?   100,000   R/S
No. CFS = ?   1   R/S
CF CHANGES ?   N   R/S
Now calculating — will take a few minutes.

IRR = 7,586.40%   IRR = Rate of Return

GROUP 2   CF AMT is the 1st-year total death benefit.

CLEAR DISPLAY. You must reenter program.

Calculate the Rate of Return for Premium Payment

Five (5) Year Measurement

ON — XEQ — ALPHA — SIZE — ALPHA — 021
XEQ — ALPHA — IRR — ALPHA
CLR ?   R/S
GROUPS ?   R/S
TOTL GROUPS =?   2   R/S
GROUP 1 CF AMT = ?   1,301   CHS   R/S
NO. CFS = ?   5   R/S
GROUP 2 CF AMT = ?   103,301   R/S
NO. CFS = ?   1   R/S
CF CHANGES ?   N   R/S
Now calculating — will take a few minutes.

IRR = 112.05%   IRR = Rate of Return

GROUP 2 CF AMT is the 5th-year total death benefit.

CLEAR DISPLAY. You must reenter program.

Fifteen (15) Year Measurement

ON — XEQ — ALPHA — SIZE — ALPHA — 023
XEQ — ALPHA — IRR — ALPHA
CLR ?   R/S
GROUPS ?   R/S
TOTL GROUPS = ?   3   R/S
GROUP 1 CF AMT = ?   1,301   CHS   R/S
NO. CFS = ?   9   R/S
GROUP 2 CF AMT = ?   0   R/S
NO. CFS = ?   6   R/S
GROUP 3 CF AMT = ?   103,554   R/S
NO. CFS = ?   1   R/S
CF CHANGES ?   N   R/S
Now calculating — will take a few minutes.

IRR = 20.65%   IRR = Rate of Return

GROUP 3 CF AMT is the 15th-year total death benefit.

CLEAR DISPLAY. You must reenter program.

Life Insurance: Its Rate of Return

Thirty (30) Year Measurement
ON — XEQ — ALPHA — SIZE — ALPHA — 023
XEQ — ALPHA — IRR — ALPHA
CLR ?   R/S
GROUPS ?   R/S
TOTL GROUPS = ?   3   R/S
GROUP 1 CF AMT = ?   1,301   CHS   R/S
NO. CFS = ?   9   R/S
GROUP 2 CF AMT = ?   0   R/S
NO. CFS = ?   21   R/S
GROUP 3 CF AMT = ?   134,213   R/S
NO. CFS = ?   1   R/S
CF CHANGES ?   N   R/S
Now calculating — will take a few minutes.

IRR = 9.71%   IRR = Rate of Return

GROUP 3 CF AMT is the 30th-year total death benefit.

CLEAR DISPLAY. You must reenter program.

Forty-five (45) Year Measurement
ON — XEQ — ALPHA — SIZE — ALPHA — 023
XEQ — ALPHA — IRR — ALPHA
CLR ?   R/S
GROUPS ?   R/S
TOTL GROUPS = ?   3   R/S
GROUP 1 CF AMT = ?   1,301   CHS   R/S
NO. CFS = ?   9   R/S
GROUP 2 CF AMT = ?   0   R/S
NO. CFS = ?   36   R/S
GROUP 3 CF AMT = ?   261,401   R/S
NO. CFS = ?   1   R/S
CF CHANGES ?   N   R/S
Now calculating — will take a few minutes.

IRR = 7.82%   IRR = Rate of Return

GROUP 3 CF AMT is the 45th-year total death benefit.

CLEAR DISPLAY.

Calculate the Rate of Return for Premium Payment

HOW TO CALCULATE THE INSURED'S RATE OF RETURN FOR WHOLE LIFE (ORDINARY LIFE) METHOD OF PREMIUM PAYMENT

Premium Offset/Vanishing Premium

Note: You calculate the insured's rate of return in the exact manner as the beneficiary's rate of return. However, use the figures for total cash value as the future value to the insured.

One (1) Year Measurement

It is not necessary to do this calculation as the future value to the insured is zero (0) and the rate of return is −100% compound.

Program: IRR

Five (5) Year Measurement

ON — XEQ — ALPHA — SIZE — ALPHA — 021
XEQ — ALPHA — IRR — ALPHA
CLR ?   R/S
GROUPS ?   R/S
TOTL GROUPS =?   2   R/S
GROUP 1 CF AMT = ?   1,301   CHS   R/S
NO. CFS = ?   5   R/S
GROUP 2 CF AMT = ?   5,660   R/S
NO. CFS = ?   1   R/S
CF CHANGES ?   N   R/S
Now calculating — will take a few minutes.

IRR = −4.60%   IRR = Rate of Return

GROUP 2 CF AMT is the 5th-year total cash value.

CLEAR DISPLAY. You must reenter program.

Life Insurance: Its Rate of Return

Fifteen (15) Year Measurement
ON — XEQ — ALPHA — SIZE — ALPHA — 023
XEQ — ALPHA — IRR — ALPHA
CLR ?   R/S
GROUPS ?   R/S
TOTL GROUPS = ?   3   R/S
GROUP 1 CF AMT = ?   1,301   CHS   R/S
NO. CFS = ?   9   R/S
GROUP 2 CF AMT = ?   0   R/S
NO. CFS = ?   t   R/S
GROUP 3 CF AMT = ?   21,047   R/S
NO. CFS = ?   1   R/S
CF CHANGES?   N   R/S
Now calculating — will take a few minutes.

IRR = 5.39%   IRR = Rate of Return

GROUP 3 CF AMT is the 15th-year total cash value.

CLEAR DISPLAY. You must reenter program.

Thirty (30) Year Measurement
ON — XEQ — ALPHA — SIZE — ALPHA — 023
XEQ — ALPHA — IRR — ALPHA
CLR ?   R/S
GROUPS ?   R/S
TOTL GROUPS = ?   3   R/S
GROUP 1 CF AMT = ?   1,301   CHS   R/S
NO. CFS = ?   9   R/S
GROUP 2 CF AMT = ?   0   R/S
NO. CFS = ?   21   R/S
GROUP 3 CF AMT = ?   63,186   R/S
NO. CFS = ?   1   R/S
CF CHANGES ?   N   R/S
Now calculating — will take a few minutes.

IRR = 6.64%   IRR = Rate of Return

GROUP 3 CF AMT is the 30th-year total cash value.

CLEAR DISPLAY. You must reenter program.

Calculate the Rate of Return for Premium Payment

Forty-five (45) Year Measurement

ON — XEQ — ALPHA — SIZE — ALPHA — 023
XEQ — ALPHA — IRR — ALPHA
CLR ?   R/S
GROUPS ?   R/S
TOTL GROUPS = ?   3   R/S
GROUP 1 CF AMT = ?   1,301   CHS   R/S
NO. CFS = ?   9   R/S
GROUP 2 CF AMT = ?   0   R/S
NO. CFS = ?   36   R/S
GROUP 3 CF AMT = ?   187,016   R/S
NO. CFS = ?   1   R/S
CF CHANGES ?   N   R/S
Now calculating — will take a few minutes.

IRR = 6.95%   IRR = Rate of Return

GROUP 3 CF AMT is the 45th-year total cash value.

CLEAR DISPLAY.

Life Insurance: Its Rate of Return

PREMIUM OFFSET ILLUSTRATION

Plan: ORDINARY LIFE +
Issue Age: 35 MALE
Class: PREFERRED STANDARD

Annual Premium: $1,301.00
P.A.C. Premium: $112.20
Face Amount: $100,000

Policy Year	Premium Payable*	Cash Premium Payment*	Guaranteed Cash Value	Total Cash Value*	Annual Increase In Total Cash Value*	Cash Prem (−) Total Cash Value Increase*	Dividend Adds Death Benefit*	Total Death Benefit*
1	1,301	1,301	0	0	0	1,301	0	100,000
2	1,301	1,301	1,215	1,274	1,274	27	313	100,313
3	1,301	1,301	2,438	2,620	1,346	−45	929	100,929
4	1,301	1,301	3,699	4,080	1,460	−159	1,858	101,858
5	1,301	1,301	4,997	5,660	1,580	−279	3,101	103,101
6	1,301	1,301	6,330	7,369	1,709	−408	4,664	104,664
7	1,301	1,301	7,699	9,222	1,853	−552	6,554	106,554
8	1,301	1,301	9,104	11,228	2,006	−705	8,775	108,775
9	1,301	1,301	10,545	13,403	2,175	−874	11,334	111,334
10	539	0	12,022	14,459	1,056	−1,056	9,283	109,283
11	479	0	13,534	15,592	1,133	−1,133	7,529	107,529
12	415	0	15,081	16,807	1,215	−1,215	6,070	106,070
13	346	0	16,660	18,109	1,302	−1,302	4,899	104,899
14	258	0	18,271	19,519	1,410	−1,410	4,061	104,061
15	162	0	19,912	21,047	1,528	−1,528	3,554	103,554
16	68	0	21,581	22,692	1,645	−1,645	3,349	103,598
17	−25	0	23,276	24,454	1,762	−1,762	3,421	103,950
18	−125	0	24,997	26,343	1,889	−1,889	3,770	104,620
19	−226	0	26,742	28,363	2,020	−2,020	4,380	105,592

Calculate the Rate of Return for Premium Payment

20	−334	0	28,509				106,869
21	−448	0	30,297	30,523	2,160	−2,160	5,251
22	−594	0	32,103	32,830	2,307	−2,307	6,378
23	−742	0	33,925	35,317	2,487	−2,487	7,822
24	−902	0	35,759	37,991	2,674	−2,674	9,567
25	−1,075	0	37,603	40,863	2,872	−2,872	11,620
26	−1,262	0	39,454	43,949	3,086	−3,086	13,990
27	−1,466	0	41,308	47,266	3,317	−3,317	16,686
28	−1,684	0	43,163	50,830	3,564	−3,564	19,721
29	−1,916	0	45,016	54,660	3,830	−3,830	23,104
30	−2,166	0	46,863	58,772	4,112	−4,112	26,842
31	−2,437	0	48,699	63,186	4,414	−4,414	30,949
32	−2,732	0	50,518	67,920	4,734	−4,734	35,442
33	−3,062	0	52,315	72,999	5,079	−5,079	40,344
34	−3,424	0	54,082	78,456	5,457	−5,457	45,697
35	−3,820	0	55,816	84,320	5,864	−5,864	51,533
36	−4,248	0	57,515	90,622	6,302	−6,302	57,886
37	−4,710	0	59,182	97,397	6,775	−6,775	64,787
38	−5,205	0	60,825	104,684	7,287	−7,287	72,267
39	−5,727	0	62,449	112,533	7,849	−7,849	80,356
40	−6,278	0	64,060	120,984	8,451	−8,451	89,070
41	−6,863	0	65,656	130,083	9,099	−9,099	98,429
42	−7,500	0	67,232	139,874	9,791	−9,791	108,459
43	−8,200	0	68,778	150,411	10,537	−10,537	119,207
44	−8,962	0	70,283	161,747	11,336	−11,336	130,738
45	−9,795	0	71,736	173,933	12,186	−12,186	143,113
				187,016	13,083	−13,083	156,401

New England Mutual Life Insurance Company

Life Insurance: Its Rate of Return

Summary #	Guaranteed Cash Value	Total Cash Value*	Cash Premium Payments	Premium Payments Less Total Cash Value*	Guaranteed Paid-up Insurance	Total Paid-up Insurance*
5 years	4997	6036	6505	469	17754	21447
10 Years	12022	15381	11709	3672–	35929	45968
15 Years	19912	22573	11709	10864–	50503	57252
20 Years	28509	34410	11709	22701–	62072	74920
Age 65	46863	70783	11709	59074–	78352	118345

Terminal Dividend* 15th yr: $249.00 20th yr: $2067.00

Interest-Adjusted Indexes* based on a 5.00% interest rate, for basic policy only:

Life Insurance Net Payment Cost Index	10 yrs: $9.85	20 yrs: $6.80	Age 65: $3.96
Life Insurance Surrender Cost Index	10 yrs: $0.75	20 yrs: $2.00–	Age 65: $3.24–
Equivalent Level Annual Dividend	10 yrs: $3.16	20 yrs: $6.21	Age 65: $9.05

Premium Information:	Annual	Semi-annual	Quarterly	Monthly	P.A.C.
ORDINARY LIFE	$1,301.00	$666.95	$338.56	$114.45	$112.20

The cash premium payments illustrated may be pre-paid with a single payment of $9,709.

Calculate the Rate of Return for Premium Payment

Dividends* used to purchase paid-up insurance years 1 thru 9. Thereafter, dividends are used to reduce premiums and, if necessary, a portion of the paid-up insurance is surrendered to pay the balance of the premium. Dividend Additions Death Benefit reaches its lowest point in year 16. Illustrated dividends assume no loans on the policy. Policy loans will reduce dividends.

* Includes dividend values. Dividends are a return of part of the premium and primarily depend on investment earnings, mortality and expense experience. Dividends are computed on current dividend scale and are neither guarantees nor estimates for the future. A Terminal Dividend is payable upon surrender, lapse or death, after at least 15 policy years, but only if declared by the Company at such time, and is included in the Total Death Benefit, in Summary Values for Total Cash Value and Total Paid-up insurance and in the Interest-Adjusted Surrender Cost Index.

+ The values shown in the ledger assume an annual mode of premium payment and a(n) 8.00% policy loan interest rate. The issuance of any policies or riders is subject to the Company's regular underwriting practices. The amounts of coverage and premiums for any policies or riders, if issued, may differ from those illustrated.

Summary Values are calculated as of the end of the year.

New England Mutual Life Insurance Company

Appendix

TEST YOURSELF: RATE OF RETURN QUIZZES AND ANSWERS

Life Insurance: Its Rate of Return

Case Study Quiz Number 1[1]

A male, 45-years-old, has been told by his banker to purchase $500,000 of term life insurance to cover his bank loan for five years. The life insurance will only be needed for five years. Two plans have been presented:

Plan "A" Annual Premium		Plan "B" Annual Premium	
Year 1	$825.00	Year 1	$525.00
Year 2	975.00	Year 2	1,075.00
Year 3	1,200.00	Year 3	1,300.00
Year 4	1,510.00	Year 4	1,610.00
Year 5	1,660.00	Year 5	1,860.00

Life insurance agent "A" says his plan should be purchased because over the five-year period his plan has a total premium outlay of $6,170.00 versus $6,370.00 for Plan "B." Life insurance agent "B" says even though his plan has a total premium outlay of $6,370.00 versus $6,170.00, the rate of return is higher on his plan. Assuming death occurs in the 5th-year, what is the rate of return for Plan "A" and what is the rate of return for Plan "B"?

---

[1] These are typical questions that, Life Insurance: Its Rate of Return, and the Brownlie Method of Calculations attempt to answer.

Case Study Quiz Number 2

A 52-year-old male is the subject. His father purchased $5,000 of Whole Life for him in 1947. The premium is $104.90 annually (the policy is guaranteed cost). The current cash value of the policy is $3,298.25.

The insured's life insurance agent, who is skilled in the area of rate of return, has told the insured that his beneficiary's rate of return is 0.62% if the insured dies at the age of 65, which is 13 years away.

Is the agent correct? Figure the beneficiary's rate of return.

Life Insurance: Its Rate of Return

Case Study Quiz Number 3

A 50-year-old male, non-cigarette smoker, is considering the purchase of $64,000 of Whole Life (Ordinary Life) using dividends as declared to purchase additional paid-up life insurance.

The man has narrowed his choice to two plans ... either Massachusetts Savings Bank Life Insurance or New England Mutual Life. He does not intend to borrow on the policy and wishes to have the policy mature as a death benefit.

Massachusetts Savings Bank Life Insurance Ledger Statement, dated 12/28/82 indicates:

Premium: $1,735.68 (does not include premium waiver)

Total Death Benefit:		
	Year 5	$66,399
	Year 10	73,627
	Year 15	84,597
	Year 20	99,095

New England Mutual Life Insurance Company Ledger Statement, dated 12/17/82 indicates:

Premium: $1,568.04 (does not include premium waiver)

Total Death Benefit:		
	Year 5	$ 65,555
	Year 10	72,282
	Year 15	86,434
	Year 20	108,649

Appendix: Test Yourself

The proposed insured has told the life insurance agent from New England Mutual Life that the Massachusetts Savings Bank said the Interest-Adjusted Cost Index is the only way to compare policies.

Massachusetts Savings Bank Life Insurance Interest-Adjusted net cost at 5% per $1,000 of insurance

Year 5	6.15%
Year 10	5.21%
Year 15	4.92%
Year 20	4.91%

New England Mutual Life Interest-Adjusted net cost at 5% per $1,000 of insurance

Year 5	Not shown
Year 10	3.83%
Year 15	1.89%
Year 20	0.32%

The agent from New England Mutual Life is asked to explain what the index means in simple terms. The agent responds that he does not understand the Interest-Adjusted Index.

Based upon the information from the official ledger statements provided in this case study, calculate the beneficiary's rate of return for 5 years, 10 years, 15 years and 20 years.

Life Insurance: Its Rate of Return

Plan: WHOLE LIFE DIV-OP
Issue Age: 50 MALE

Annual Premium: $1,735.68
Face Amount: $ 64,000

End Of Year	Guaranteed Cash Value	Dividend Additions*	Cash Value Of Dividend Additions*	Total Death Benefit*	Cash Value Including Dividends*
1	1,312.00	154	62.08	64,154	1,374.08
5	6,721.92	2,399	1,092.75	66,399	7,814.67
10	13,751.68	9,627	5,028.57	73,627	18,780.25
20	28,495.36	35,095	23,250.10	99,095	51,745.46
Age 65	20,996.48	20,597	12,177.16	84,597	33,173.64

Summary	Guaranteed Cash Value	Cash Value of Dividend Additions*	Less Premiums Paid	Difference (–Less; + More)	Interest-Adjusted Net Cost (5%)** (Per $1000)
5 Years	6,721.92	1,092.75	8,678.40	– 863.73	6.15
10 Years	13,751.68	5,028.57	17,356.80	+ 1,423.45	5.21
20 Years	28,495.36	23,250.10	34,713.60	+17,031.86	4.91
Age 65	20,996.48	12,177.16	26,035.20	+ 7,138.44	4.92

Summary	Guaranteed Paid-up Value	+Dividend Paid-up Value	Total Paid-up Value
5 Years	14,784	2,399	17,183
10 Years	26,368	9,627	35,995
20 Years	43,072	35,095	78,167
Age 65	35,520	20,597	56,117

Appendix: Test Yourself

By using the Dividend Cash Value, the insurance could be made paid-up for $64,640, exceeding the face amount after 17 years under the current dividend scale.*

Premium does not include optional charge for waiver of premium benefit $72.32.

* All dividends are based on the current dividend scale now being paid by all savings and insurance banks. Future dividends depend on future experience and cannot be guaranteed.

** The Interest-Adjusted method recognizes the time value of money in arriving at net cost. Under this method, the cost of life insurance is the value of the premiums less the cash surrender value and the value of dividends, using a 5% interest factor as required by regulations. Other presentations of net cost or gain illustrated above do not recognize that, because of interest, a dollar in the future has less value than a dollar today.

Savings Bank Life Insurance

Life Insurance: Its Rate of Return

STANDARD LEDGER STATEMENT

Plan: ORDINARY LIFE+
Issue Age: 50 MALE
Class: PREFERRED STANDARD

Annual Premium: $1,568.04
P.A.C. Premium: $135.96
Face Amount: $64,000

Policy Year	Guaranteed Cash Value	Total Cash Value*	Annual Increase In Total Cash Value*	Premium Less Total Cash Value Increase*	Dividend Adds Death Benefit*	Total Death Benefit*
1	0	0	0	1,568	0	64,000
2	1,431	1,480	1,480	88	143	64,143
3	2,834	2,990	1,510	58	438	64,438
4	4,257	4,591	1,601	33–	903	64,903
5	5,698	6,294	1,703	135–	1,555	65,555
6	7,156	8,115	1,821	253–	2,414	66,414
7	8,630	10,067	1,952	384–	3,496	67,496
8	10,115	12,164	2,097	529–	4,822	68,822
9	11,611	14,426	2,262	694–	6,410	70,410
10	13,115	16,872	2,446	878–	8,282	72,282
11	14,624	19,520	2,648	1,080–	10,457	74,457
12	16,136	22,392	2,872	1,304–	12,956	76,956
13	17,649	25,513	3,121	1,553–	15,803	79,803
14	19,160	28,876	3,363	1,795–	18,958	82,958
15	20,666	32,498	3,622	2,054–	22,434	86,434
16	22,163	36,383	3,885	2,317–	26,221	90,221

17	23,647	40,540	4,157	2,589–	94,316
18	25,112	44,986	4,446	2,878–	98,741
19	26,554	49,738	4,752	3,184–	103,511
20	27,967	54,814	5,076	3,508–	108,649
21	29,353	60,237	5,423	3,855–	114,171
22	30,713	66,057	5,820	4,252–	120,133
23	32,052	72,322	6,265	4,697–	126,581
24	33,377	79,071	6,749	5,181–	133,530
25	34,691	86,336	7,265	5,697–	140,993
26	35,992	94,152	7,816	6,248–	148,992
27	37,277	102,565	8,413	6,845–	157,566
28	38,538	111,619	9,054	7,486–	166,771
29	39,765	121,356	9,737	8,169–	176,656
30	40,950	131,810	10,454	8,886–	187,270
Age 65	20,666	32,498	3,622	2,054–	86,434

* Illustrated dividends assume no loans on the policy. Policy loans will reduce dividends. Dividends used to purchase additional paid-up insurance.

New England Mutual Life Insurance

Life Insurance: Its Rate of Return

Summary #	Guaranteed Cash Value	Total Cash Value*	Total Premium Payments	Total Premiums Less Total Cash Value*	Guaranteed Paid-up Insurance	Total Paid-up Insurance*
5 Years	5,698	6,657	7,840	1,183	12,406	14,493
10 Years	13,115	18,011	15,680	2,331–	24,835	34,106
15 Years	20,666	35,145	23,521	11,624–	34,552	58,759
20 Years	27,967	60,564	31,361	29,203–	42,004	90,963
Age 65	20,666	35,145	23,521	11,624–	34,552	58,759

Terminal Dividend* 15th yr: $258.56   20th yr: $1713.28

Interest-Adjusted Indexes* based on a 5.00% interest rate, for basic policy only:

Life Insurance Net Payment Cost Index	10 yrs: $19.35	20 yrs: $13.68	Age 65: $16.32
Life Insurance Surrender Cost Index	10 yrs: $ 3.83	20 yrs: $ 0.32	Age 65: $ 1.89
Equivalent Level Annual Dividend	10 yrs: $ 5.15	20 yrs: $10.82	Age 65: $ 8.18

Premium Information

	Annual	Semi-annual	Quarterly	Monthly	P.A.C.
ORDINARY LIFE	$1,568.04	$803.81	$407.99	$137.82	$135.96

* Includes dividend values. Dividends are a return of part of the premium and primarily depend on investment earnings, mortality and expense experience. Dividends are computed on current dividend scale and are neither guarantees nor estimates for the future. A Terminal Dividend is payable upon surrender, lapse or death, after at least 15 policy years, but only if declared by the Company at such time, and is included in Summary Values for Total Cash Value and Total Paid-up Insurance, and in the Interest-Adjusted Surrender Cost Index.

+ The values shown in the ledger assume an annual mode of premium payment and a(n) 8.00% policy loan interest rate. The issuance of any policies or riders is subject to the Company's regular underwriting practices. The amounts of coverage and premiums for any policies or riders, if issued, may differ from those illustrated.

Summary Values are calculated as of the end of the year.
New England Mutual Life Insurance Company

Appendix: Test Yourself

Case Study Quiz Number 4

Compare the Salomon Brothers, Inc. compounded annual rates of return and answer the following questions:

Compounded Annual Reates of Return

	15 Years	Rank	10 Years	Rank	5 Years	Rank	1 Year	Rank
Oil	20.4%	1	25.4%	2	16.2%	4	−14.7%	15
U.S. Coins	17.9%	2	25.7%	1	13.2%	6	16.8%	5
U.S. Stamps	16.8%	3	19.2%	3	21.8%	1	−6.2%	14
Gold	16.6%	4	15.5%	5	17.5%	3	28.6%	4
Chinese Ceramics	14.2%	5	4.0%	14	13.1%	7	0.0%	11
Silver	12.6%	6	17.3%	4	19.7%	2	109.5%	1
Diamonds	10.1%	7	10.3%	7	5.4%	13	0.0%	10
Farmland	10.0%	8	11.7%	6	7.0%	12	−5.7%	13
Treasury Bills	8.8%	9	10.1%	8	12.8%	8	10.8%	6
Housing	8.6%	10	9.2%	9	7.4%	10	2.1%	8
Old Masters	7.8%	11	8.4%	10	4.1%	14	1.7%	9
CPI	7.3%	12	8.5%	11	9.1%	9	3.9%	7
Bonds	6.4%	13	6.6%	13	7.2%	11	39.0%	3
Stocks	5.7%	14	7.5%	12	14.8%	5	51.8%	2
Foreign Exchange	3.1%	15	1.4%	15	−2.8%	15	−4.3%	12

All returns are for the period ended June 1, 1983, based on latest available data.
Source: Salomon Brothers, Inc.

1. Do any of the compounded rates of return in the Salomon Brothers, Inc. table equal and/or exceed the beneficiary's rate of return for the life insurance plans and/or methods of premium payments for 1 year, 5 years and 15 years shown in this book?

2. Do any of the compounded rates of return in the Salomon Brothers, Inc. table equal and/or exceed the insured's rate of return for the life insurance plans and/or methods of premium payments for 1 year, 5 years and 15 years shown in this book?

Life Insurance: Its Rate of Return

Answers to Case Studies

Case Study Quiz Number 1
    Plan "A" Beneficiary's rate of return is 229.48%
    Plan "B" Beneficiary's rate of return is 246.98%

Case Study Quiz Number 2
    Yes! The insurance agent is correct. The rate of return is 0.62%.

Case Study Quiz Number 3
    Massachusetts Savings Bank Life Insurance

Year 5	77.72%
Year 10	25.35%
Year 15	13.72%
Year 20	9.19%

    New England Mutual Life Insurance Company

Year 5	81.68%
Year 10	26.80%
Year 15	15.08%
Year 20	10.77%

Appendix: Test Yourself

Case Study Quiz Number 4

1. No.

2. Yes, all do for 1 year and 5 years.
   For 15 years all do but Foreign Exchange.

Note: Please keep in mind that life insurance proceeds payable to the beneficiary are not subject to Federal Income Tax. The beneficiary's rates of return shown in this book are *net* rates of return.

The compounded annual rates of return shown in the Salomon Brothers, Inc. table are *gross* rates of return before taxes. For a person in the 40% tax bracket the rates of return have to be reduced by 40% for non-capital gains investments, and 16% for capital gains investments.